Material Culture of the Orissan Tribals

An Illustrated Study of
Kutia, Dongaria and Malia Kondhs

Material Culture of the Orissan Tribals

An Illustrated Study of Kutia, Dongaria and Malia Kondhs

Nityananda Patnaik

D.K. Printworld (P) Ltd.
New Delhi

Cataloging in Publication Data — DK
[Courtesy: D.K. Agencies (P) Ltd. <docinfo@dkagencies.com>]

Patnaik, N. (Nityananda), 1926-
Material culture of the Orissan tribals : an illustrated study of Kutia, Dongaria and Malia Kondhs / Nityananda Patnaik.
xi, 207 p. 23 cm.
Includes bibliographical references (p.)
ISBN 8124604223 (hb)

1. Kandh (Indic people) — Material culture — India — Orissa. 2. Kutia Kondh (Indic people) — Material culture — India — Orissa. 3. Dongria Kondh (Indic people) — Material culture — India — Orissa. I. Title.

DDC 305.891 456 22

ISBN 81-246-0422-3 (Hardbound)
ISBN 81-246-0423-1 (Paperback)

First published in India in 2007

Published and printed by:
D.K. Printworld (P) Ltd.
Regd. office : *'Srikunj'*, F-52, Bali Nagar
Ramesh Nagar Metro Station
New Delhi - 110 015
Phones : (011) 545 3975; 546 6019
Fax : (011) 546 5926
E-mail: dkprintworld@vsnl.net
Website: www.dkprintworld.com

Preface

THE present report is a study on the Material Culture of the Sub-groups of the Kondh tribe of Orissa. A study of all aspects of the material side of people's life is of great importance. It is of great interest from such points of view as forms and functions of artefacts, sources of invention, questions of diffusion and their relation to social organization, religion and ceremonial practices. The scientists find it very useful in anthropological inquiry of tribal and other communities. A deep knowledge about the material life of a community is an excellent way of gaining the confidence of people and establishing rapport with them for data collection and field investigations among them.

The artefacts, art objects and such other items of material culture are an integral part of other aspects of a culture. Taking all material items of a culture together make the material culture of a community. There may be considerable similarities in form and function of material items from place to place, in a particular community, be it a peasant community or a tribal community. There may also be differences in form and function of certain material items from place to place, in a particular community, and such local differentiations are largely due to cross-cultural contact and acculturation.

It is assumed that the material culture of a community may be the same in respect of the various items which comprise the material culture in different localities. But under the influence of geographical conditions and acculturation, there appears to be spectacular changes and discordances in form and function of the material items which constitute the material culture of a particular community. This book deals with the material culture of the Kondh tribe. The Kondhs are divided into three sub-groups, namely the Kutia Kondh — inhabiting the Belghar region of Phulbani district, the Dongaria Kondhs — occupying Niyamgiri hills of Koraput district, and the Malia Kondhs of Sadar sub-division of Phulbani district. There appear to be considerable similarities in socio-cultural, religious and aesthetics aspects and belief-system laws regarding social control and world-view of the sub-groups which accord to the traditional Kondh culture pattern. But as one goes down to the base representing the material culture we notice greater differences in the material level of life. Thus the structure of a society can be compared to a pyramid. There is more differentiation at the material base of the social system and progressively less as one mounts higher and higher. The differences at the material aspects of culture are eventually replaced by a unity of beliefs and aspirations which gives to the community in question a character of its own. In other words, the study of the material culture of a society reveals unity in diversity in its local system and culture pattern.

Nityananda Patnaik

Contents

PART II
Dongaria Kondhs of Koraput and Kalahandi Districts

PART III
Malia Kondhs of Phulbani District

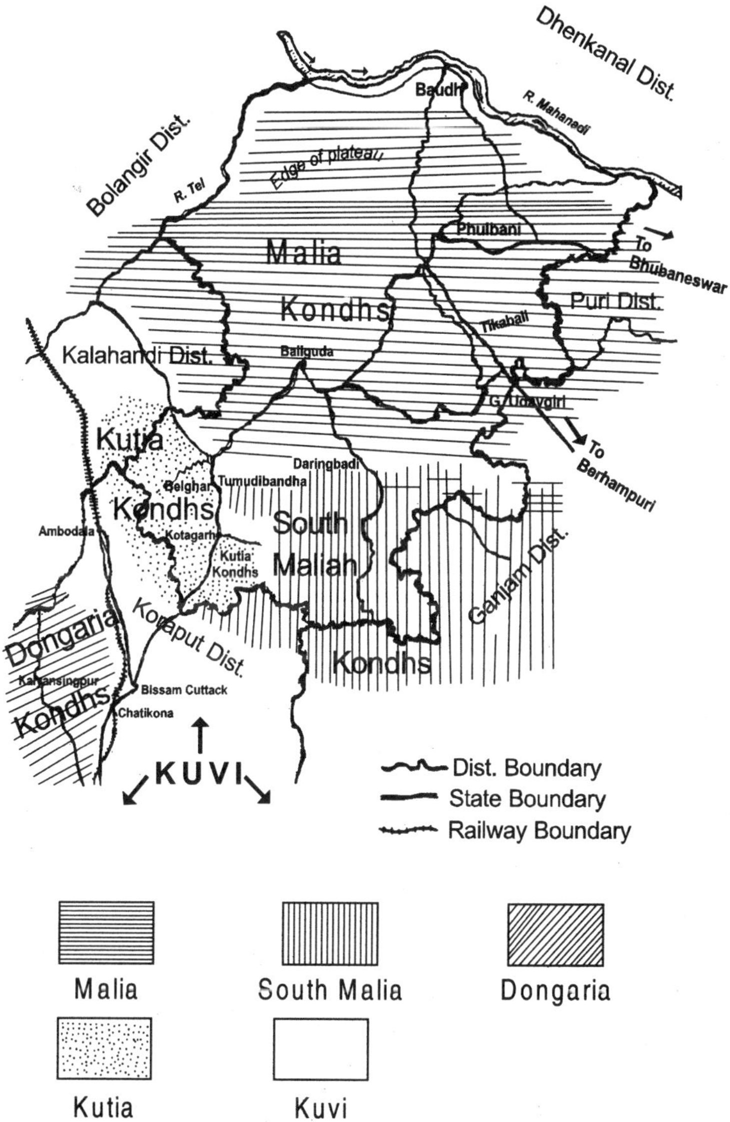

Map showing the area of study.

General Introduction

THE introduction comprises two parts, namely: (1) A short account of the Kondhs in general, and (2) An introductory sketch of human habitation. As the book relates to the Kondhs, it is necessary to give an account of the cultural and social aspects and some other special features of the Kondhs. Moreover, of all aspects of material culture, the aspect concerning human habitation and settlement pattern is the most important. Therefore, it is necessary to give a short account of this aspect which is of great variety in form and function.

The Kondh in general

The Kondh is a major tribal community of Orissa. According to the 1981 census, their population was 9,89,342. They are distributed in almost all districts of Orissa, but their concentration is in Koraput, Kalahandi and Phulbani districts. Formerly there were 13 districts in the State, but recently the number has increased to 30 districts. Since the population figures of the Kondhs of all these 30 districts are not available, figures of the Kondhs of the old 13 districts, as per the 1981 census, is given in Table 1.

Table 1: Districtwise Kondh population, as per 1981 census

District	*Population*
Sambalpur	30693
Sundergarh	2184
Keonjhar	1214
Mayurbhanj	197
Balasore	197

Cuttack	5805
Dhenkanal	26501
Phulbani	251633
Bolangir	71386
Kalahandi	129749
Koraput	369231
Ganjam	63848
Puri	36704
Total	989342

The Kondh tribe was famous for its pernicious practice of human sacrifice called *Mariah* and female infanticide. These practices were abolished during British time and since then buffalo sacrifice known as *Kedu* festival is being practised in place of human sacrifice. The tribe comprises mainly three sub-groups, namely the Kutia Kondhs — inhabiting largely the Belghar area of Phulbani district; the Dongaria Kondhs — living largely in Niyamgiri hill ranges covering Kalyansinghpur, Bissamcuttack and Muniguda areas of Koraput district, besides the Lanjigarh hills of Kalahandi district; and the Malia Kondhs — inhabiting Phulbani district. Besides these sub-groups there are Kondhs in the plains of other districts and they are generally called Desia Kondhs.

The Kondhs have a language of their own with two dialects. The Kui-speaking Kondhs inhabit Phulbani district and the Kuvi-speaking Kondhs are found in Koraput district. Those living in the plains of other districts have forgotten their mother tongue and have adopted Oriya language.

The habitat of the Kutia and Dongaria Kondhs is mountainous and therefore rugged, uneven and undulating terrain covered with thick forest. But the Malia country is relatively less hilly and therefore less rocky and rugged. Although these groups belong to the same large Kondh tribe they are isolated from each other due to physical barriers and therefore they are not thought to have come from a common region which is located somewhere in the southern part of the country. They are dispersed in different directions and live in different localities. They finally landed up in the habitats where they are now found separated from one another leading their life as independent groups.

Since these sub-groups had a common origin and later branched off from their parent community they had many cultural elements in common. But, as they lost contact with one another due to physical barriers, their culture started changing in course of time under the influence of nature and cultural contact with other communities. The interplay of many factors mainly the terrain, natural resources, environment and cultural contact with their neighbouring communities contributed to change in their original culture pattern and moulded them to become distinct independent groups.

Several studies on acculturation have shown that different aspects of culture do not change uniformly. Some aspects are changing more while some are changing less. The degree of change in different aspects depends upon varying interplay of change agents. The general picture of the dynamics of change is that the hardcore of culture changes least and other parts change most. In the study of *Peasant Life in India, A Study in Indian Unity and Diversity*, what N.K. Bose had stated in the Introduction, is reproduced below:

> What is even more assuring is that, as one considers other spheres of life, namely, things like laws which guide inheritance or define the rights and duties of individuals in a kind group, or if one rises to higher reaches of life confined to ideals or faiths or art, the differences which one has noticed at the material level of life gradually become feeble and feebler. They are eventually replaced by unity of beliefs and aspirations which gives to Indian civilization a character of its own.

He has further added that,

> The structure of Indian unity can, therefore, be compared to a pyramid. There is more differentiation at the material base of life and progressively less as one mounts higher and higher.

> It is needless to say that the implication is not that village people are more different from one another than city people or sophisticated and propertied classes; but that whether it is a village or a dweller of an Indian town, there is more variety in regard to some aspects of life and less in relation to others.

In this book not all aspects of Kondh culture have been discussed to show what aspects have changed most and what aspects have changed least among these three sub-groups of the Kondh tribe. The discussion is confined to the material sphere of their life and the comparative picture of this sphere of their life. These three sub-groups show what forms different items of material culture have taken and what factors have possibly worked to give the particular items such shapes and forms. Both aspects of this problem namely the continuity of original shape and change in shape have been discussed to show to what extent these sub-groups look alike and to what extent they have drifted from each other.

The book covers the following items of material culture to show the continuity and change in this sphere. Broadly they are as follows:

1. Human habitation, settlement pattern and house types
2. Household material objects
3. Basketry
4. Food quest
5. Personal care, dress and adornments
6. Musical instruments
7. Religious materials

Human Habitation and Settlement Patterns and House Types

By habitation, it means that it is a place of abode with physical environment. More than the physical aspect of a locality and the communities inhabiting, it refers to all aspects which a culture subsumes. In fact, the pattern of habitation is determined by the interplay of mutual influence of both physical and cultural factors. Besides physical characteristics, the religion, mythology, cosmology, customs, traditions, and social groupings of a community have each a hand in patterning its habitation.

Likewise the criteria for the selection of a site for founding a human habitation, the land use pattern, composition of population, layout of houses and settlement pattern in a particular habitation are all determined by social and cultural factors. The cosmos may be reflected in the whole range of structural and functional phenomena starting from the forms of settlement or villages to the house types, even to the space allotted for different functions within a house, one and all speaking of the world-view of the community. In other words, the habitation may be regarded as a miniature of universe of a community.

SETTLEMENT PATTERN

The settlement pattern takes different forms depending upon their physical setting and location and also upon socio-cultural and economic consideration. Some of these different forms are:

(1) *Shapeless Cluster*

This type has mainly two variations, one of massive type and the other of dispersed type. In both the cases no regular village street is present except a tortuous path growing out of people's movement.

(2) *Linear Cluster*

It has rows of houses with a common village street in between. There may be a single pair of parallel rows with houses facing each other on either side of the village street or several such rows.

(3) *Square or Rectangular Cluster*

The settlements having multiple parallel rows of houses take either a square form or a rectangular form with streets running parallel or at right angles to one another.

(4) *Isolated Cluster*

Villages formed of isolated Sahis or streets, a number of which makes a settlement reckoned as a Mauza in revenue records.

The question arises as to why some settlements are compact and others are dispersed. Many factors are involved — physical, social and economic — as well as other factors related to culture and religion. The tribal villages, particularly those found in the hills, conform mostly to dispersed pattern — there is very little plain land in the hilly terrain which is undulating and slopy. To build houses adjacent to one another in a line is inhibited by the rugged and tortuous terrain. Individual houses are built in a dispersed manner conforming to a shapeless cluster. Since the tribal people are cohesive and depend upon mutual help in all spheres of their life the shapeless massive cluster of houses outnumber the far-flung dispersed houses.

Within the massive cluster of houses in a village there are separate sub-clusters inhabited by discrete lineage groups. And in some cases the houses in such settlements are built so close to one another, that the pattern looks like that of nucleated village in which houses are nucleated around a specific point or a central place. The place may be *Mandaghar* (bachelor's dormitory) or the shrine of the village deity (*Gramshri*) as in the case of the Juangs of Orissa. Among the Bondas of Koraput district, the village conforms to a shapeless compact cluster. But since the houses are built closely, dispersed on different terraces of a site, it gives some sort of arranged or ordered appearances. There is nothing special in the central point around which the closely spaced houses are nucleated.

The examples of linear villages or street villages are many. Such types are found where sufficient plain surface is available. The individual houses which are built along the straight street are either close to one another having absolutely no space in between or separated from each other with each having a compound around the house. The settlement pattern noticed among the Kutia or Dongaria Kondhs of Orissa coincides with the former category and that among the Santals in some areas to the latter category. In both the cases there is nothing like nucleation around any spot, but there is a point of focus in each of these linear types. In the case of the Kondhs, the *Dharani Penu* (Goddess of Earth) is installed in the street at a central place and in the case of the Santals the residence of *manjhi hadam* (secular headman) is located at a place central to the village in one of the rows of houses. As the ancestors of *manjhi hadam* are believed to hover around the central place, the entire street is held sacred. Similarly, the location of the shrine of *Dharani Penu* in the village street among the Kondhs has made it sacred. In both the cases, even though the alignment of houses is of linear pattern, all houses not having a nucleated origin have an eye on the centre.

PART I

Kutia Kondhs of Phulbani District

1

A Brief Ethnographic Account of the Kutia Kondhs

THE Kutia Kondhs, a little known tribe of Orissa, lives in the remote hills of extreme south-west of Phulbani district as well as adjoining parts of the Kalahandi district. They occupy Tumudibandha and Kotagarh blocks of Phulbani district and Thuamul Rampur area of neighbouring Kalahandi district.

The areas inhabited by them is situated at about 3,500 ft above sea level and comprises forest-clad hills interspersed with rivers and perennial streams. The area lies roughly on 12°45' E longitude.

Though the population figures of different sub-groups of Kondh tribe have not been separately assessed, the enumeration done by Kutia Kondh Development Agency, Belghar in a group of 70 villages, arrived at a figure of 4,090.

The Kutias speak *Kui* language and most of them understand Oriya because of their contact with the neighbouring people in the weekly markets of Belghar, Tumudibandha and Ambadola.

The socio-economic and cultural life of Kutia Kondh revolves around the forest environment. They practise slash and burn cultivation on the hill slopes, taking special care to protect medicinal plants and fruit-bearing trees. The slopes of the upper part are used for raising pulses and the lower region for growing ragi, maize and small millets. Vegetables and tubers are also grown in the middle zone of the hill slopes. A particular patch is used for three years at a stretch and left fallow for more than five years. Where they have plain valley table-land with perennial water streams nearby paddy is also grown. In the kitchen garden adjoining to homestead they use cowdung manure and grow tobacco, mustard and gourds.

From sowing operation in the months of May and June to sequential harvesting in the months of November and December both men and women work in the swidden fields. The agricultural operations like weeding, transplanting, reaping and collection of corns which need much concentration are mostly performed by women along with other household chores like husking, plastering of walls and kitchen chores.

Bamboo and *sal* timber are the two most frequently used items of the Kutias. In the construction of houses bamboo and *sal* timber are the principal materials. Most of the males are skilled in bamboo work and prepare door shutters, grain containers, mats, fishing traps and baskets of different sizes.

The forest gives shelter to several animals like sambar, barha, kutra, and deer, which provide them food. Due to denudation of forest the hunting activities of Kutias are nowadays restricted.

The food of Kutia is influenced by the environment. In general they take food once in the morning, followed by a midday meal and a meal late in the evening. The meals comprise ragi gruel, maize, millets, rice, green leaves, vegetables as well as dry fish and meat. As beverages they take brewed rice beer and mohua liquor and *salap* of sago palm.

The economic life of the Kutia Kondh is largely influenced by the forest. Throughout the year they collect mushrooms, green leaves, roots, tubers, fruits and seeds as per seasonal availability. Denudation of forest has resulted in scarcity of minor forest produce like lac, gum, honey, hill broom, fibre, etc. The shortage of food in the lean period, payment of bride price, expensive marriage feasts, natural calamities, annual cycle of festivals and socio-religious obligations put the Kutia Kondh always in financial crisis.

Family is the smallest social unit among the Kutia Kondhs. It is mostly nuclear, patrilocal, patrilineal and patriarchal in character. Family lineage among the Kutia Kondhs plays an important role in uniting the people for several socio-cultural and economic functions.

Clan unity among the Kutia Kondhs is quite prominent and unique for its structure and socio-cultural functions. In earlier days Kutia Kondh villages were uniclan villages, but nowadays the villages have become multiclan in composition.

The Kutia Kondhs have a strong village organization. The *mutha majhi* who was in charge of collecting revenue from the people of the *Mutha* in olden days belonged to *Paik* caste. The *pat majhi* is the formal head of the *Mutha* coming next to the *mutha majhi*. *Mutha* comprises a number of villages. The *chhatia* is a man who belongs to the *Pano* community and serves as a messenger-cum-cattle herder. Jani, the magico-religious head commands great respect in the village.

The Kutia Kondh women wear many kinds of beautiful golden and silver ornaments with different designs. Almost each part of their body is adorned with ornaments. They wear rings in ears, nose and fingers, hair clip, bead necklaces, bangles, waist band, etc. to decorate their body. The females also put on two pieces of cloth one around the waist and the other wrapped around the upper half of the body. They cut the sarees into three pieces and use the pieces for a long time.

The weapons used by the Kutia Kondhs mostly are arrows, axes, adzes and knives. The agricultural implements include pick and mattock, hoe, spade, crowbar, plough, yoke, leveller and sickle. The musical instruments like flute and single membrane drum, violin, etc. are in use among them. They use several types of baskets made of bamboo-splits. Various earthenware pots are bought from the potters of the locality for use as cooking vessels and water pots.

The magico-religious performances are associated with several sacrifices. Such festivals as *Meria* sacrifice, *Punikalu*, *Takupuja*, and *Padar Puja* are very important. The most important among them is the *Meria* festival when buffalo is sacrificed and offered by the community to the Mother Earth (*Dharani Penu*). At the individual or family level, goat, chicken and pigeon are sacrificed. After this short account of the Kutia Kondhs there follows description of different items of material culture in the same order as mentioned in the introduction.

2

Human Habitation, Settlement Pattern and House Types

THE Kutia Kondhs live in villages in which houses are built in two contiguous rows facing each other. The houses are identical but vary in size depending upon the economic standard and number of family members. The number of houses varies from five to fifty. As the village is built on gentle hill slopes, the front verandah of a house overlooking each other runs continuously from upper slope to the lower slope.

The village street which is fairly wide, runs in-between both the rows. The rainwater is drained out of the village through this street. The surface of the street is quite uneven throughout its length and breadth. Somewhere in the middle of the street the Goddess Earth (*Dharani Penu*) is installed.

When a village is over-populated, resulting in population pressure on homestead and agricultural lands, some families leave the village and start living in new settlements which come up nearby. Establishment of new settlements is also thought of when the Kutias feel a particular place responsible for the cause of suffering and natural calamities.

For selecting a new place, the villagers study the area from several angles keeping in view the major criteria like high and elevated landscape, availability of perennial streams nearby, luxuriant forest growth all around for shifting cultivation and for collection of forest resources for food, fodder and house construction materials.

The next step after selection is the magico-religious performance. The villagers summon the diviner (*kataku*) for conducting a special kind of ritual. Coconut and *Mahuli* liquor are offered and a pig or fowl is sacrificed before *Dharani Penu*. Then *Kataku* is possessed by the spirit of the Goddess Earth and while in trance tells people whether the place is auspicious or not. In the new place, thus selected, the village elders distribute homestead lands as well as swidden plots among different households keeping in view the need of different families.

The village street is always situated in east-west direction as the Kutia believes that "Sun" is the guardian of all deities and spirits and directs them all for the wellbeing of the village. The powerful sunlight washes away all evils and the sunlight is shared by each house equally. In the village, the *Jani* occupies one row of the village and the *majhi* occupies the opposite row facing the *Jani's* row. It is believed that *Jani's* household should always be situated face to face with the God, viz. *Pijurudangar*, the range of hills in front.

House Types

GROUND PLAN

The ground plan of a Kutia house is a multi-roomed complex and rectangular in shape. There is a small pathway just at the entrance to the house which leads to the main living room. On either side of the pathway a verandah is raised. These elevated platforms (*dapa*) are sometimes box type or rectangular in shape. The family members, after strenuous work in the agricultural fields, sit here comfortably and spend time chit-chatting with the neighbours. All the households are lined in a row and it is a continuous verandah running from one end to the other so that the house owners of two extreme ends can talk to each other sitting in their respective verandahs. In some households, verandah is used for keeping large baskets containing food grains. This is also used as a place for meeting the visiting guests and outsiders. Two or three mortar holes are fixed on the ground in almost all verandahs for pounding paddy. A rope-woven cot finds its place in the verandah. In summer days, male members and guests sleep in this enclosure which gets sufficient sunlight through the door and a small opening acting as window in the wall. The housewife prefers this place for combing her hair, and for processing foodstuffs

View of Rangaparu village and adjoining paddy fields.

Settlement pattern : View of Rangaparu village.

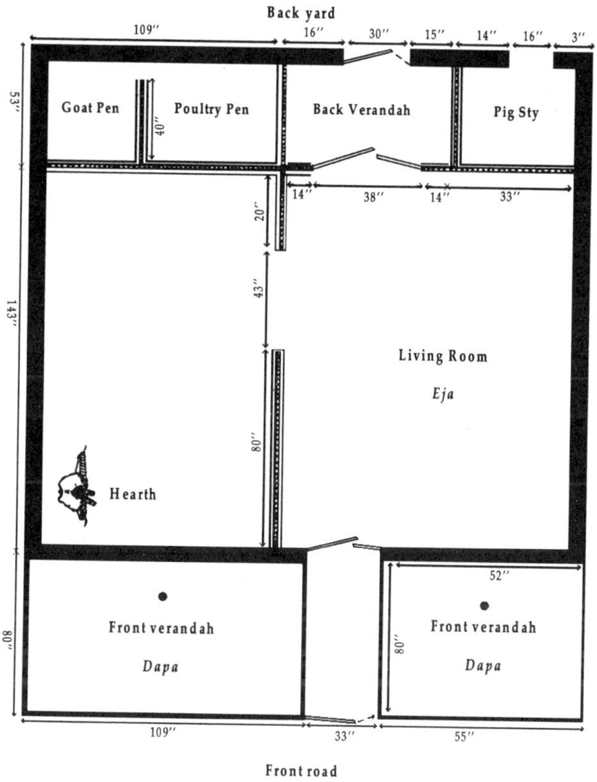

Ground plan of a Kutia Kondh house.

collected from forest and agricultural fields. In many houses, a flat wooden board fixed in the verandah wall serves as lamp stand.

Bahar Tati (Shutter at the Entrance)

The main entrance to the house has no permanently fixed door. A shutter made of bamboo splits interwoven horizontally and vertically (*tati*) is being fixed to a bamboo pole to serve as a door at the entrance.

Front view of a tiled thatched house.

Front view of a straw thatched house.

Different Types of Windows

***Eja* (Living Room) and *Vitrieja* (Kitchen)**

The entrance to the living room is provided with a strong double panelled wooden door (*behari deba*) fixed to the wooden frame made of *sal* wood. This door is provided with clamp and chain to keep the door locked when needed. Previously these doors were made by outside carpenters. Nowadays the young Kutia boys can prepare good doors out of *sal* wood fetched from the forest free of cost. Wooden benches and stools are set in position in the living room on which baskets containing food grains and seeds are kept. In the space below the platform, an oven is made for preparation of some food at times when needed. In addition the hearth gives warmth and helps the inmates to spend time comfortably particularly in winter nights.

In the living room all the family members sleep and dine. They use mats and cots for sleeping. Male members usually sleep on cots. In the living room curry stones of different sizes are kept which are meant for crushing food grains, spices and tobacco leaves. On the walls are hung dry gourds of different sizes in which grains used during rituals are preserved. From the ceiling (*attu*), bamboo poles are

Inside view of living room.

suspended horizontally which serve as clothes hangers. Maize seed corns tied together in line are kept hanging from such bamboo poles. Wherever there is shortage of space in the living room, the grain bins are shifted to the loft overhead.

A partition wall divides the living room into two portions; the kitchen occupies the smaller, and the living section occupies the larger portion. There is a door provided in the partition wall which opens towards the kitchen which has no other opening and, therefore, it is dark inside. The fireplace (hearth) is usually located in the corner of the kitchen, away from the door. The smoke which emits from the

Inside view of Kitchen room.

fireplace goes up and passes out through the tiles with which the roof is covered.

In the kitchen, opposite to the hearth, a platform of required size is provided adjoining the partition wall. On this platform water vessels and vessels containing food are kept.

View of back verandah.

Jaka (Back Verandah)

Coming out of the living room through a back door (*akagiri deba*) one notices two verandahs, same as the front verandah, flanked by a narrow passage leading from the living room. Then comes the backyard. One of the verandahs which is enclosed is used by ladies and adolescent girls during their period of menstruation.

The females are not allowed to use other rooms during menstruation period and the male member does the cooking. They are not allowed to come to the street in front as the abode of Goddess Earth (*Dharani Penu*) is

Side view of front verandah.

Side view of front verandah.

present there, lest there be mishap and misery caused by the deity in fury.

The other verandah is used in almost all houses as the shed for livestock, pigs, goats, hens, etc. The back door of the house is made of bamboo wicker work and is fixed to a pole which helps to open and close it when needed.

The Kutias grow vegetables in the backyard and some creeper plants are trailed on scaffolds raised temporarily. In the backyard, fire-wood, timber and other building materials are stored. Cow sheds are also located in the backyard and cows, bullocks and buffaloes of two to three neighbours are kept in a common shed.

Construction of a House

A house to be constructed requires 15 to 20 strong poles of *sal* wood of varying lengths. As many as four poles from the central line hold the ridge beam. Next three lines of pillars are posted on either side of the central poles. The central poles are 10' in height and the poles of the side lines starting from the line adjoining to the central line to the last line are respectively in descending order 7', 4'-7" and 2'-5" in height on which the rafters are laid on both the slopes.

View of a Kutia Kondh house.

On the rafters rest the wooden planks leaving a gap of about 6" in-between. About 25 pieces of planks are required for a common house. The planks are fixed to the beams by using iron nails. A layer of mud is spread on the planks and in this mud plaster clay tiles are fixed. An ordinary house requires about 6000 tiles for the roof.

Khapars (Clay Tiles for the Roof)

A man can make 600 clay tiles per day. The work usually is carried out near a pond or a stream. The *khapars* are dried and then burnt. Previously, the local potters were supplying *khapars* to the Kutias but nowadays almost every Kutia male knows how to make *khapars* for his use.

Loft Overhead

Loft (*papi*) in the house is constructed just at a man's height in the living room (*eja*). Wooden planks are placed side by side resting over the eastern and western side walls. A mud coating is given on the surface of the loft. It is a place for storing grains and household materials. A small opening is left near the door overhead for approaching the loft by a ladder.

Side wall of a house.

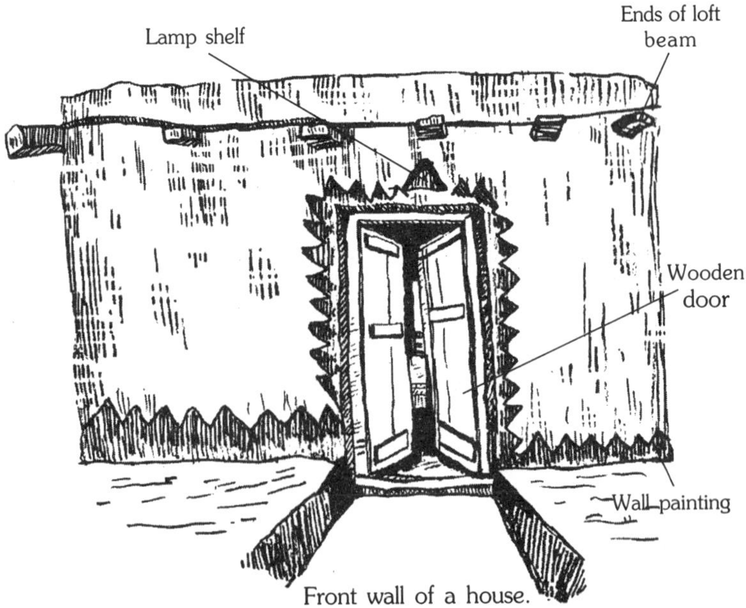

Front wall of a house.

Construction of Walls

For construction of walls, the earth dug out from the foundation is used. The walls are also stone-packed and mud plastered. To make the walls smooth a mud plaster is given and it is the work of the women. Nowadays wattle walls of bamboo splits are rarely seen and no house is provided with windows. The doorframes are set in position when walls are constructed and the doors which are fixed to these frames are given a coating of red earth collected from ant hills. This is just for the sake of decoration and nothing else.

Construction of Doors

The doors are double-panelled and fitted to the doorframe by three hinges. The wooden frames and panels are made of *sal* (*Sargi*) wood.

Wooden doors.

The door is made by a carpenter or by a Kutia male. Three to four pieces of wooden planks are fixed side by side by iron nails. The door is provided with latches and chains for locking.

Tati (Shutters)

Some shutters are made of bamboo splits and are used for various purposes in Kutia houses. It is used as door shutters at the entrance and exit of the house. It is also used as a base for keeping large grainbins on it. After applying a coating of cow dung over the *tati,* it

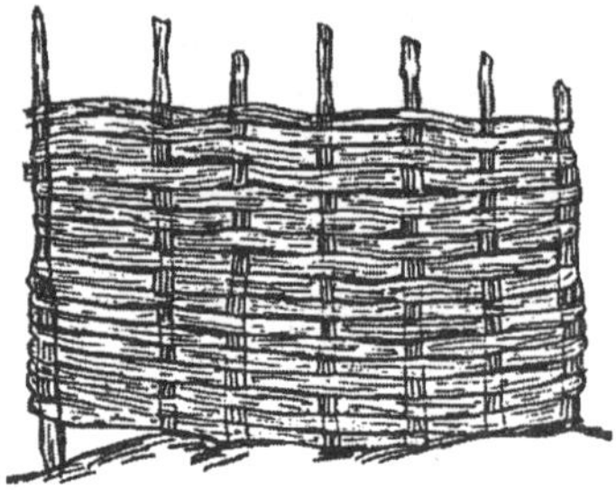

Maning Bei (*Fence*)
Check pattern.

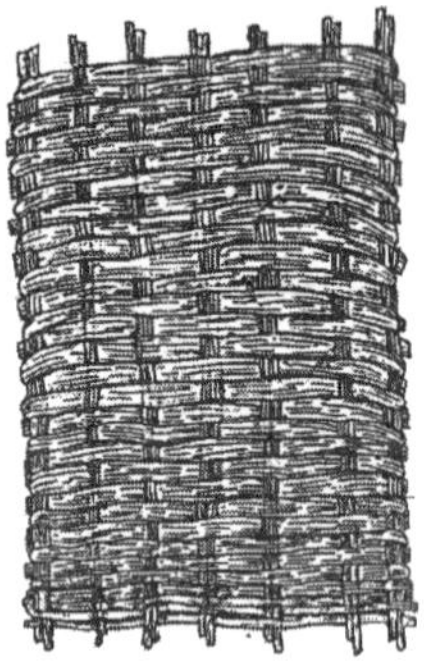

Maning Bei (*Fence*)
Check pattern.

is placed on a loft over which the grainbins are kept. The *tati* is used for making walls of the house. The bamboo mat is plastered with mud on both sides to make it durable and strong. The bamboo mats are multipurpose, these are used to make enclosures for cattle shed, pig sty and goat pen.

Pajing Soleng (Pig Sty)

Pajing Soleng (Pig Sty).

Wooden trough in which feed is given to pigs.

It is constructed close to the house. It is open in front and the wooden poles are used to make walls.

***Kaju, Ada Ilu* (Goat and Poultry Pen)**

These huts are more massive than pig stys.

Goat and Poultry Pen.

***Koding Sala* (Cowshed)**

The cowshed has enclosures on all sides and thatched with straw.

Cowshed.

***Asang Gurudu* (Duck pen)**

The duck pen is an enclosed hut. The walls are made of bamboo mats. The shutter is also made of a piece of bamboo mat.

Duckpen.

Wall and Floor Designs

Wall design.

The Kutias express their love for beauty by decorating the walls and floor of the house with floral and geometric designs. Zigzag bands, a series of close triangles, criss-cross lines, floral drawings, parallel straight or wave-like lines are some of the examples by which doors and floors of the house are decorated. They are equally skilled in wood carving of various types. The wooden poles which support the roof and doors exhibit carvings of various types. These designs or motifs are only for decoration purposes and have no ritual significance. They exhibit a strong incentive to artistic activity.

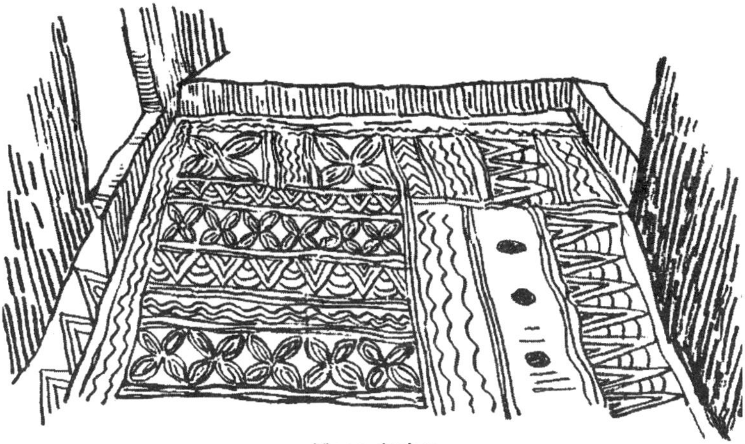

Floor design.

At the entrance of a house, a line of paddy grains arranged in a string is hung overhead to add beauty to the house.

***Daska Kudi* (Spinsters' Dormitory)**

Every *Kutia* village has more than one hut used as spinsters' dormitory (*daska kudi*). Generally these huts are located in the back of the

Spinsters' Dormitory.

rows of houses. It is a single roomed house with the roof sloped to one side and thatched with grass. The walls are made of bamboo

mats and a wooden door is provided which serves both as entrance and exit.

Dehu Penu and *Dharani Penu* (Shrines)

There are two shrines one at the entrance of the village for *Dehu Penu* (deity guarding the village) and the other in the middle of the village for *Dharani Penu* (Mother Earth). Three stone slabs resting on a piece of flat stone represent the deity *Dharani Penu* which is installed in a hut which has four engraved wooden poles on which a two-sided gabled roof thatched with country earthen tiles rests. *Dehu Penu* is represented by a piece of flat stone lying on the ground under the roof with an earthen pot and small pieces of stones which

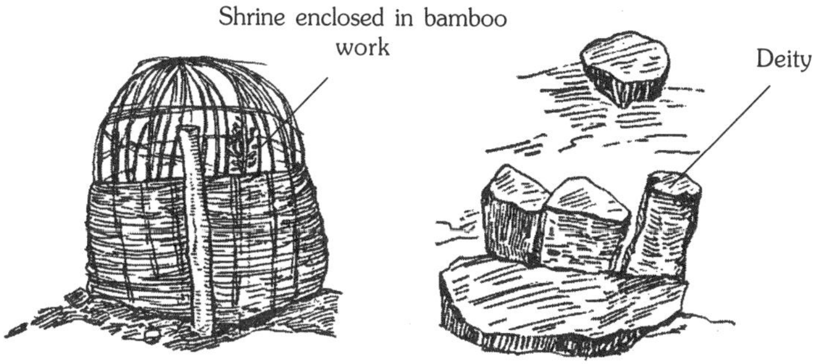

Dehu Penu Dharani Bali

Shrine at the middle of the village.

Dehu Penu Dehu Penu

Shrine at the entrance of the village.

are used at the time of worship. The symbol of the deity is represented by a woodwork resting high above at the back end of the roof.

***Pabaveru/Jagdi* (Field Huts)**

Field huts are built in the swidden fields and other places to keep watch over standing crops. Men, and not women, use this hut at night as well as in day time scaring away birds and animals so that crops are not destroyed.

The huts are built both on the ground and on a tree. Where no suitable tree is available, the hut is built on a raised platform for the sake of safety. Generally the hut is of gabled type and its sides are closed while the front and the back are kept open. The hut is made of wooden poles and mats. Sometimes branches are used to cover the sides and the top of the hut.

Certain musical instruments like flute and drums are kept to play as well as make sound to scare away the animals. On the floor under the hut, the fire is kept alight and the watchman comes down and sits by its side for warmth.

As human habitation is determined by social and cultural factors, likewise the shape and size of a house is influenced by the same socio-cultural factors. House types differ from tribe to tribe, caste to caste, and locality to locality. Materials used for construction, the height of the building, alignment of rooms, uses to which different parts of a house are put, are all governed by human, environmental and physical factors. The doors and windows to be made are also prescribed by cultural norms and resources of the area. Apart from these factors, prestige and position of houseowners play a very important role in the shape and size of the house. Briefly, it can be summed up that the type of a house of any human group always forms a part of its life and the house which is an important aspect of material culture is constructed not only as a material urge but as a cultural activity.

3

Household Objects

Jhatra (*Siperi* and *Prang Jhatra*) — Broom

THE *siperi* type of broom is made out of a plant called *Satrangi* — broom grass. The strands of the sticks are collected in the month of February and dried in the sun for 4-5 days. Then these are tied into small bunches by means of Siali creeper to make them fit to be used as brooms. Broom grass is a minor forest produce in the Kutia area. A broom in interior market in tribal areas costs Rs. 2 to Rs. 3 per piece whereas it costs Rs. 15 to Rs. 20 in towns.

Prang Jhatra

This broom is made out of twigs of a bushy plant (*jhatra*). The bush is uprooted in the month of November and spread in the sun. After the branches are sufficiently dried, these are collected in small bunches and tied in tough fibres. These twigs are much tougher and stronger than the broom grass and they are used in works of cowdung plastering, village street sweeping, cowshed and goat pen cleaning.

Kadeli (String Cot)

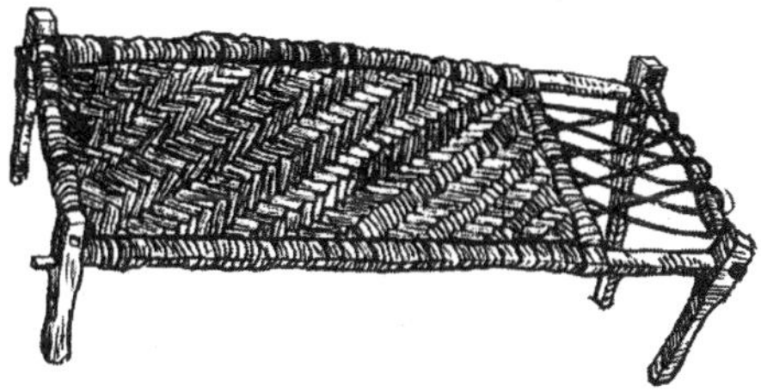

In every Kutia house there may be at least a cot which is made by the houseowner or anyone who knows how to make it. The frame is made of *damani* wood (*Grewia liciacfolia*) and the legs of *jaruki* wood (*Grewia tiliaefolia*). Strings made from siali creeper (*Bauhinia vahlii*) and from a kind of grass called *baber* (*Eulalipsis binata*) are woven to the frame to make it suitable for sleeping. The grass which grows wild are uprooted and planted in places not accessible to cattle. Planting is done in the rainy season and harvesting in winter season. The strings of siali creeper lasts for 3 or 4 years whereas those of the grass lasts longer. Generally the cot is kept out in the verandah in day time and shifted to living room at night. Men sleep on the cot while women sleep on the floor.

Phade (Stool)

The stool consists of a wooden plank and a wooden log made of *sal* wood. The plant is shaped circular and the wooden log has three small branches which are kept erect on the ground. The stool is usually placed on the floor of the verandah. While using the stool, the user places the plank on the log and sits on it.

Gunjer Bali (Quern)

The object consists of two heavy circular stones. It is made by the Doms. The user of the quern fixes it on the ground. One of the stones (*darubali*) is laid down half-buried in the ground. At the centre of it, a small wooden peg (*kuti*) is inserted into the cavity and kept tight. Another stone a bit heavier in weight is placed over it at the centre of which a hole is made. Another hole is made on the side at the upper surface of the stone (*lahabali*) and an L-shaped wooden peg is inserted into it which serves as a handle. The pegs are made of wood.

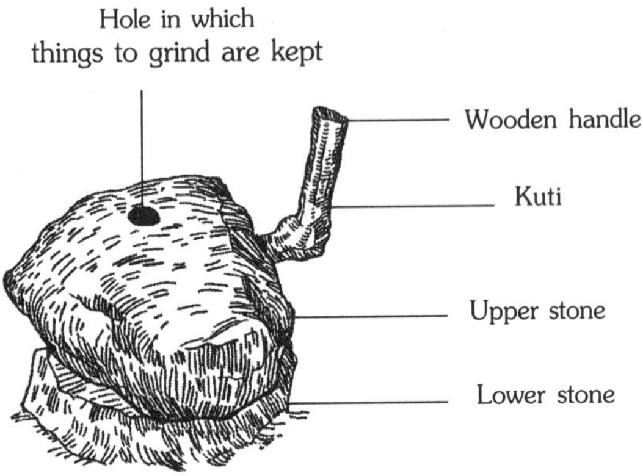

Grinding stone.

The Kutia housewife in a sitting posture inserts grains through the hole at the centre and at the same time holding the L-shaped wooden peg rotates the upper stone in clockwise direction on the lower one. The grains in between come out in powder form through the small opening between the stones.

Kallu (Pestle)

The pestle is made of a single piece of *jaruki* or *dingini* wood. The bottoms haft (*muti*) of the pestle is shaped round and smoothened by means of adze. The foreshaft (kallu) is greater in girth than the bottom portion and hexagonal in shape. At the butt end of the pestle an iron ring (*pareni*) is inserted. Different geometrical art forms are carved out on the wooden surface.

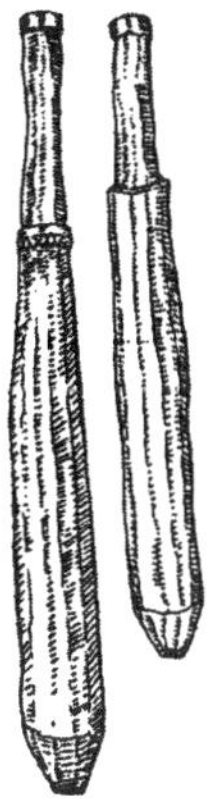

The mortar is embedded on the floor of the front verandah and main living room. The housewife while husking inserts the grains of paddy or wheat or any other grain in the mortar by one hand and pounds the grains by means of the other hand. She sits alongside the mortar spreading both of her legs on both sides of the mortar. Both the hands are used alternatively for pounding the grains.

The pestle involves no cost. Only the iron ring is purchased from the blacksmith in exchange of one kilogram of rice. The pestle lasts for ten to twelve years. Every household may have three to four pestles.

Terka Danga (A Wooden Device for Pounding Bamboo Shoots)

This food-processing implement is made of *sal* wood. It is rectangular in shape and the middle portion of it is scooped out. A small handle (*kudu*) is carved out at one end.

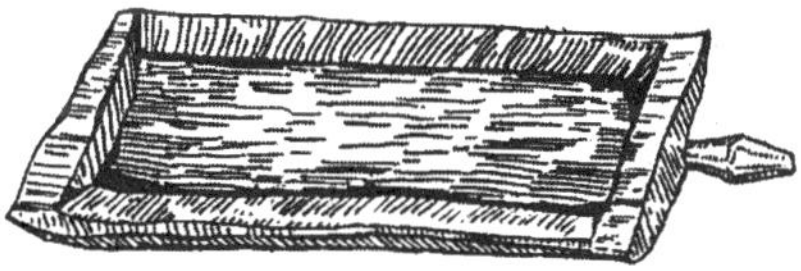

The Kutia housewife after collecting some fresh bamboo shoots cuts them into small pieces and placing them on the surface of the *terka danga,* pounds them by means of a piece of stone. The juice which comes out is thrown away and the slushy stuff obtained is fried for preparing a good dish. It is also cooked with rice.

The durability of the device is more than five years. Sometimes the bamboo shoots are consumed fresh. Otherwise these are dried and stored for future use.

Chatu (Mara Set) Ladle

The ladle is made of a wood called *jamana*. It is used for stirring rice or gruel while cooking. A narrow groove is made in the middle of the

flat portion. The handle is called *kudu,* the groove portion is called *sodanga* and the flat portion is called *set*.

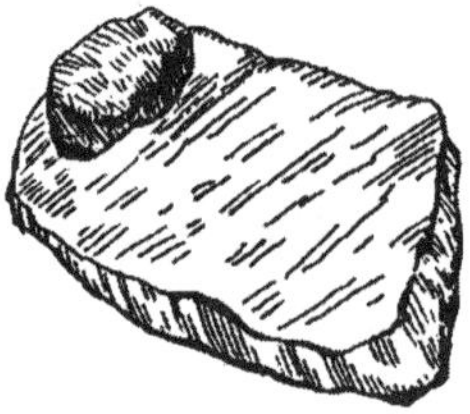

Serbebali/Merabali (Curry stone)

A piece of curry stone and a rotter also of stone are used for grinding turmeric, chilli, mustard, etc. This is the work of women.

Duabali (Stone on which Tobacco Leaves are Powdered)

The dried tobacco leaves are made into fine powder which is put into mouth. Sometimes lime is mixed in the powder.

***Nakudi Danga* (Wooden Container)**

Food is given to the dog in *nakudi danga* and pigs are given food in *Pajing Danga*.

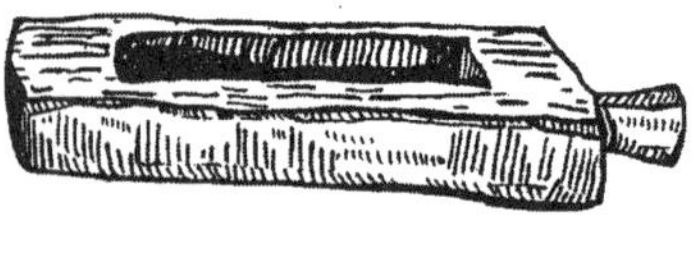

Nakudi Danga
trough from which dogs eat.

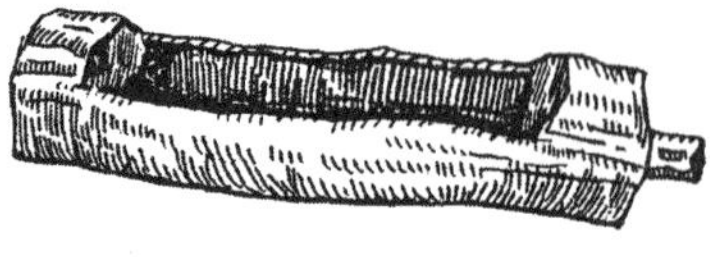

Pajing Danga
trough for feeding pigs.

These two wooden vessels are made of *sal* wood. The middle portion of the wood is scooped out to give it the form of a boat in which food is placed for the animals.

***Mani Duna* (Bamboo Container)**

The fat of the pig's stomach is kept inside this container. The older the fat the more effective it is. It has a medicinal value. It is used on the wounds caused by burning or by cutting. A liquid of black colour oozes out of the fat preserved in the bamboo container and this liquid is the medicine which is used for curing the wounds. It is fly-repellent and therefore the flies do not sit on the wounds.

***Simba Dapra* (Ladle for Serving Gruel)**

The ladle is made of a dry gourd, elongated at one end. The gourd part is cut open to make it a ladle. Gourds of different sizes and shapes are made into ladles and containers. The ladle is used for serving gruel.

Kreti (Silver ladle).

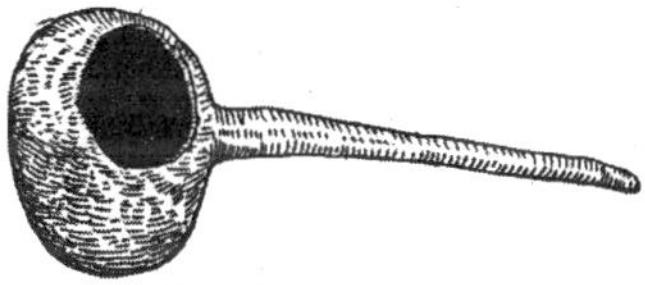

Simba dapra (ladle).

The seeds are sown during the month of May in the swidden fields as well as in the kitchen garden. A full grown gourd is plucked during the month of October. On the occasion of a festival, namely *Nuapuja* or *Punikalu*, the gourd is offered to the deity *Dharani Penu* (Mother Earth) before it is used as a ladle.

***Madang Dana* (Leaf Cup)**

The leaf cup is made of leaves from sago palm tree. Two sticks from the same tree are used in its making. A large size leaf is being folded from both the sides and stitched by the twigs obtained from the same tree to give it a cup-like shape.

Sadani tinei
(Container).

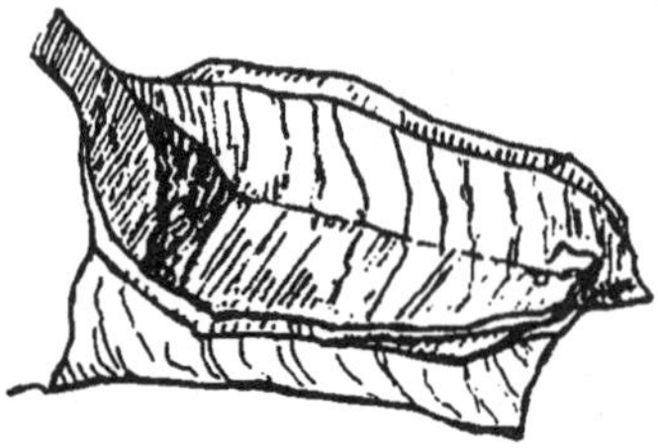

Madang dana
(Leaf cup).

The leaf cup is held by both the hands and used for drinking sago palm juice. It is also used for drinking soups and taking curries. It is usually made at the time of taking the juice. A number of cups are made at a time and kept hanging from the roof by a thread attached to it for future use.

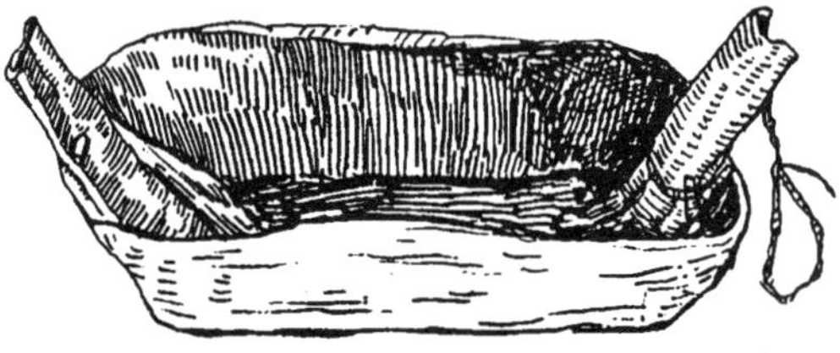

Madang dana (Leaf cup)

Dua Duna (Tobacco Container)

The container is made of a hollow piece of bamboo. After getting the bamboo from the forest its outer surface is smoothened. The bottom end of the bamboo is sealed by a joint and the upper end is kept open for keeping chewing tobacco within it. A small piece of cloth is tucked in its mouth to prevent wastage. Some of the containers are carved with different art forms with a small knife.

Usually old people, both men and women, tuck the container in their waist and carry it along with them when they go out.

During the rains, the tobacco seeds are sown in the kitchen garden and the seedlings are transplanted. The leaves are plucked during winter season and are dried for a day or two. The dry leaves are then made into powder and kept in the container. A container of average size contains as much quantity as it would last for two to three days.

***Maso Parang Titudi* (Gourd Container)**

***Minu kare* (Knife)**

***Deri kare* (Knife)**

The blade of the knife is made of iron and the handle is of wood. It is a common household article.

4

Basketry

THE native craftsmanship is exhibited in the multiformed baskets and many other household articles which even the most primitive tribes turn out with great neatness and accuracy. Braiding, intertwining, interlacing are the oldest handicrafts known to man. Basket weaving should not be confused with the art of the loom. The simple art of joining plant fibres into regular patterns to produce containers, mats and sieves comes, under the crafts of basketry. No tool is required in basketry. By far the most important braided or interwoven objects are the many and varied containers which primitive man uses to collect and store his food and belongings. They put emphasis on light weight, sturdiness and efficient shape for their woven containers. From simple interlacing to intricate spiral coil patterns the basketry exhibits craftsmanship of great excellence.

The baskets used by Kutia Kondhs are of various types and sizes. Most of them are made of bamboo splits of different thickness and strength. The Kutias make the baskets by themselves or buy them from the weekly markets. The illustrations include the following specimens.

***Kacha* (Basket)**

It is made of bamboo splits woven to conform wicker work. It is used for carrying paddy. It is plastered with cowdung so that the grains do not fall.

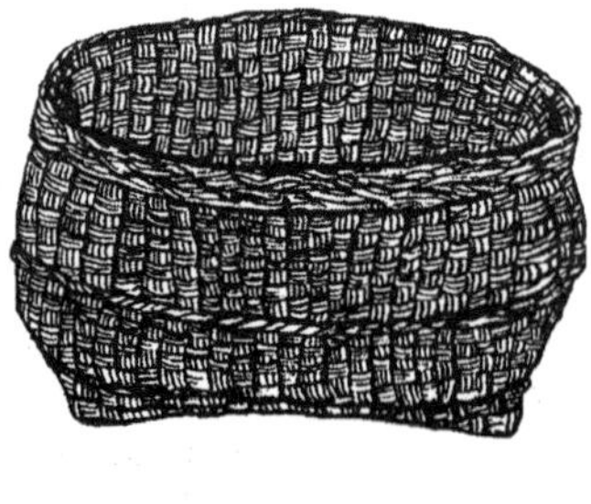

Takna **(Basket)**

It is a flat basket of wicker work of twilling pattern. It is used for drying ragi, millets and seeds of different crops and for storing grains for some time.

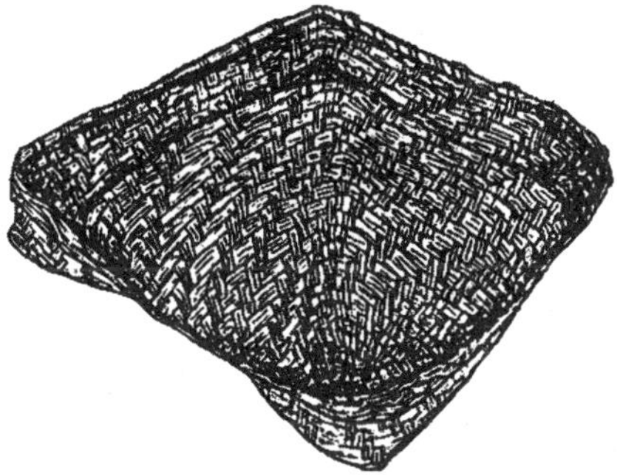

Burla **(Basket)**

A narrow mouthed small grain-bin with wicker work on the body and a coiled narrow belt providing strength to the basket.

Kulinga Gadi **(Large Grain Bin)**

It is a piece of plaited basket work of check pattern in which each weft in a circular bend passes over and then under each warp singly which in turn directs upwards. The grain bin has a mouth wide open facilitating grains to be kept inside. The wefts made of bamboo splits are uniform in size and more flexible than the warps which are tough and strong. It is used for storing food grains.

Sika Ditory **(Basket)**

It is a bag made of thin bamboo splits woven in the pattern of wicker work with coiled ropes supporting the bag. It is used for keeping small objects like coins and ornaments.

Nanka Begi **(Pellet Bag)**

The bag is made of ropes of siali creeper. The ropes are woven by means of sewing needles made out of bamboo. It is of twilling pattern. It serves as a pellet bag. The birds which destroy crops in the swidden are scared by releasing pellets with force from the string to kill them or to scare them away. While walking it is hung from the shoulder.

Sela **(Mat)**

It is a mat woven with bamboo splits. Flexible wefts pass over and under alternately to give a twilling pattern.

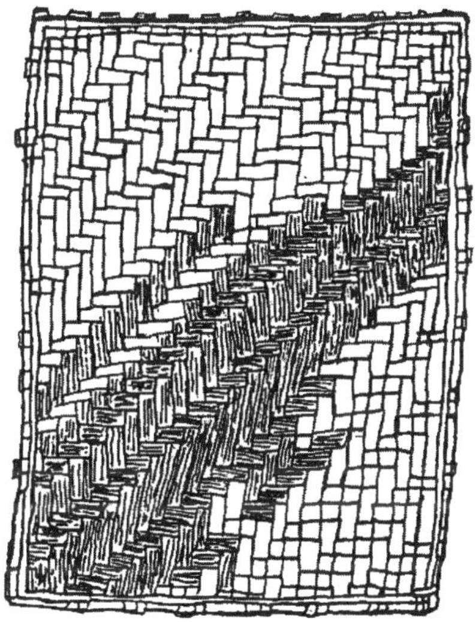

Tati **(Shutters)**

Shutter made of bamboo splits of wicker work.

Maning Bei

Fence made of thick bamboo splits showing the pattern of wicker work.

5

Food Quest

Guani (Fish Trap)

THE trap is made of slender bamboo sticks. These sticks are tied to one another in a manner so as to make it narrow at one end, bulging in the middle and tapering towards the other end. The narrow end is kept closed and the trap is kept immersed under water. The fish which makes entry into this trap under water finds it difficult to come out of it.

Sindul Duna (Gum Sticks)

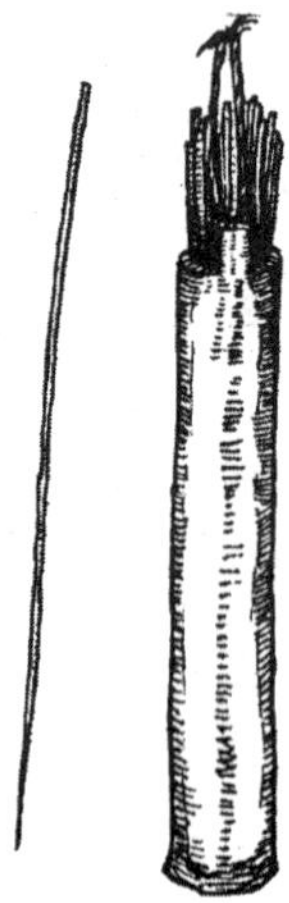

The gum sticks are used for catching birds. These are made of very thin bamboo sticks and the gums used for this purpose are collected from such trees as *tuamara*, *dumberi*, *badamara*, *bara*, *gamjumara* and *bhalia*.

The gum is applied to these tender bamboo sticks and kept inside a bamboo container having the gum inside. Locally this gum is called *sindul*. When the fruits in the banyan tree ripen and when the paddy crop is ripe birds like pigeon, parrot, etc. fly to these places to eat the fruits and the grains.

The gum-coated sticks are spread on the ground or kept on the branches of the trees. The birds which come flying to these places, to eat the fruits, come in contact with these sticks and get stuck to them rendering it difficult for them to fly away.

Kajukuting (Snare for Catching Wild Fowl)

The snare locally called *kajukuting* is used for catching wild fowl. It consists of about 25 loops made of fibres of sisal leaves. These loops are separately tied to a strong string in a line. One end of the string is tied to a stump on one side and the other to another stump on the other side. The string is kept tight and straight at a height of less than a foot above the ground. To keep the string in position, supports are provided at places along the lines. The iron ribs of a worn-out umbrella are used in required number as supports. A small loop is formed at the upper end of the rib and the end is fixed to the ground. The string passes through each rib loop from one end to the other. The rib loops hold onto the string tightly.

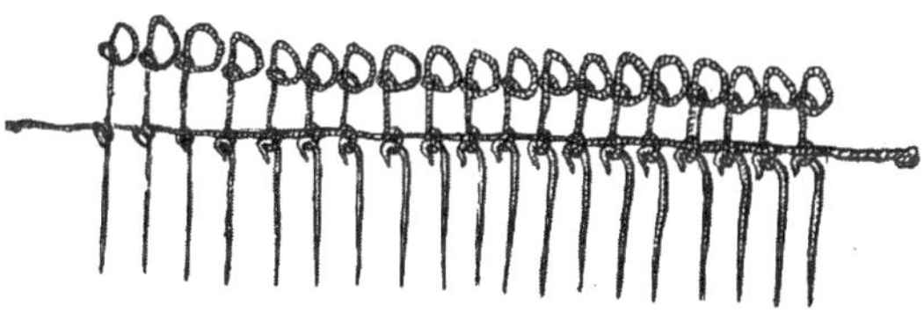

When in use, a cock is tied to the string as a bait. As the cock crows, the jungle fowls hear the sound and come running towards it for a fight. When a jungle fowl tries to attack the bait its legs get caught in the loops. As it drags the device, the loop holding the leg of the fowl gets tightened to a knot rendering it impossible for the fowl to escape.

Kaju Sipa Dituri (Birds Cage)

The pet birds are kept in the cage which is made of bamboo splits.

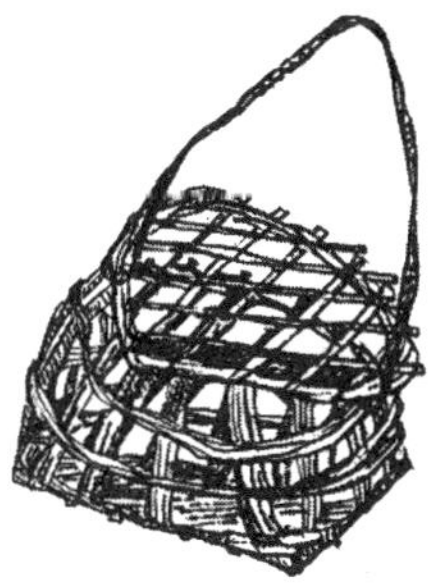

Wilu (Bow)

The bow consists of a piece of bamboo stave with notches at both ends. The fibrous tissue obtained from the neck of the buffalo or goat is made into loops which are fixed to the notches. A bamboo split is prepared to serve as a bow string (*becha*).

The bamboo string is tied to the stave at the notch by interlacing stringloops into the grove. The adjustment with regard to elasticity of the shaft is made by using the three grooves at either end. For fixing the arrow notch in the bowstring, a string notch is prepared at the centre of the bamboo string by wrapping round it the fibre retained from cocoons.

Ambu (Arrow)

The arrow consists of a slender bamboo reed (*mini*). The head (*ambu*) is a triangular piece of pointed iron-blade, both the corners below are flattened to rip up the flesh of the victim when extracted. The feathers of peacock are tied at the butt-end with cotton threads to give it a smooth flight while in use. The notch for the bow-string is cut at the butt-end of the reed.

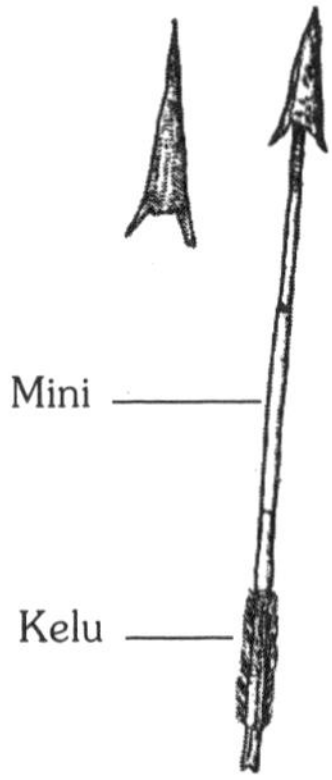

The arrowhead is made by the blacksmith and the shaft by any Kutia male. The head of arrow is inserted into the cavity of the bamboo-reed and held tight by tying it with cocoon cord. The notch at the butt end is carved out by a knife.

Langel (Plough)

The plough consists of two pieces of wood (head and body) and (beam and iron) plough share. The beam is round in shape and slightly curved. It is made of *jaruki* wood. A pointed iron share is fixed to the tapering end of the wooden head. The beam is shaped round and fixed to the body of the plough. The free end of the beam is attached to a cross-beam to which bullocks are harnessed for driving the plough. The plough lasts for three to four years.

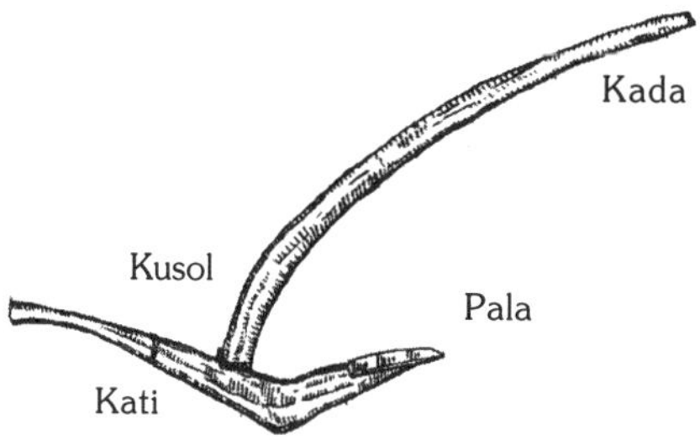

Langel (Plough).

Kadi Gutra

This is a wooden device to which the untrained bullock is harnessed. The device consists of two wooden poles. One is fixed to the ground and its free end tapers to hold the other wood having a socket at one end. Both the wooden poles are made of *sal* wood (*sargi*). The device is used for making the bullocks trained in ploughing. The bullock to be trained is tied to the horizontal beam and driven to go round and round the pole fixed to the ground.

A device by means of which bullocks are trained in ploughing.

This is kept at the outskirts of the village. Every village has got two to three such devices and it is used by any one of the village who needs it.

***Juali* (Yoke)**

The bullocks are harnessed while ploughing the field.

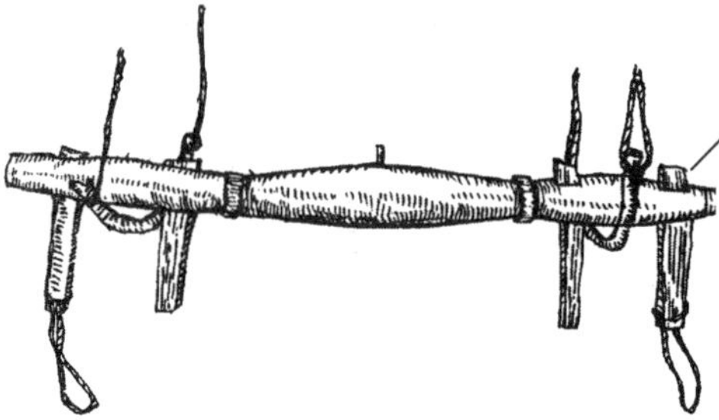

***Kurli Pade* (Leveller)**

The soil is levelled by means of *kurli* which is made of wood.

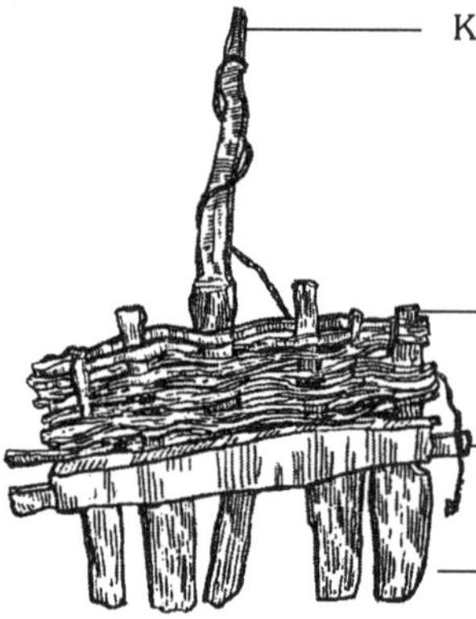

***Palka Gatra* (Sickle)**

***Pikasi* (Pick and Mattock)**

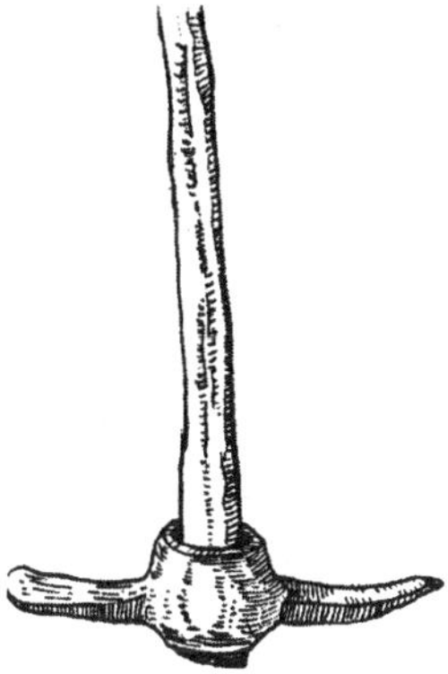

The pick and mattock consists of a handle made of *sal* wood. The handle is fixed to the socket of the tool. The pickside is pointed and the mattock edge is broad to make the blade. The iron blade is made by the blacksmith and the wooden shaft is made at home. The pick and mattock is used for digging dry and hard earth. The pick and mattock lasts for several years.

***Tangi* (Axe)**

The axe consists of a shaft (*kudi*), made of *damani* wood and a flat piece of iron blade with a sharp cutting edge. The blade has a socket at one end to which the shaft is inserted. The axe is used for sacrificing animals like buffalo, sheep, goat, etc. In almost all households this axe is kept throughout the year in a sacred place in the loft, which is considered the abode of their deities. Once in a year or two during *Meria* festival it is brought before the Goddess *Dharani Penu* for sacrificial purposes. Except on this occasion, the axe is not brought out from the loft.

***Kuradi* (Axe)**

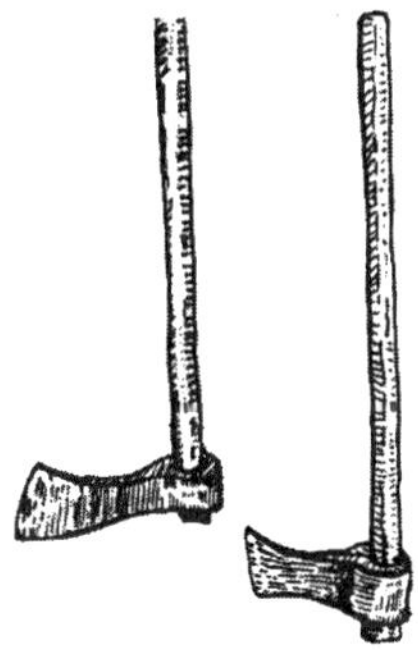

The axe consists of a wooden shaft (*kudi*) made of Damani timber and an iron blade. The iron blade has a sharp edge at one end and a socket at the other end to insert the wooden shaft. The wooden shaft is shaped round. The axe is used for cutting trees, branches and bamboos, etc. A Kutia always carries it along with him as a personal belonging to the swidden fields. He keeps the paths clean by cutting down thorny bushes, creepers, etc. by means of this axe. Usually the user carries it with its blade resting on his shoulder while the shaft hangs on the back.

***Ali Tangi* (Axe)**

The weapon consists of a wooden shaft, round shaped, made from *damani* wood and an iron blade shaped like a star with four points with a pocket at one point to which the shaft is fitted. The extreme outer part is split into two parts leaving a V-shaped opening in-between. It is a weapon specially meant for saving oneself from the attack of bears. The weapon is always carried when someone goes on a visit to his relatives, passing through the forests.

***Kepa Basuli* (Adze)**

***Tatkad* (Cow Bell)**

6

Personal Care, Dress and Adornments

Dress

A KUTIA Kondh male wears a loincloth of one and a half cubits long and less than a foot broad. This loincloth covers only the lower private part of the body. He keeps the upper part of the body uncovered. The clothes used by the Kutia Kondh women consist of three pieces. One piece covering the upper part of the body like an apron hangs in front up to the thigh. The second piece is a piece of loincloth worn between the thighs and tugged at the back to the waist string. The third piece is plain skirt worn to cover the loin. The hair is arranged into a knot at the back of the head.

The traditional customs of the Kutia Kondhs have undergone many changes. The young boys and even many adult persons have adopted modern dress like pants, trousers, shirts, etc. Similarly the young girls have replaced the upper aprons with towels. In many cases they are found wearing printed sarees and blouses. The Kutia Kondhs are very fond of wearing ornaments which are made of silver, brass, aluminium and transparent plastics. The women wear earrings and nose rings, necklaces, finger rings, anklets and toe rings.

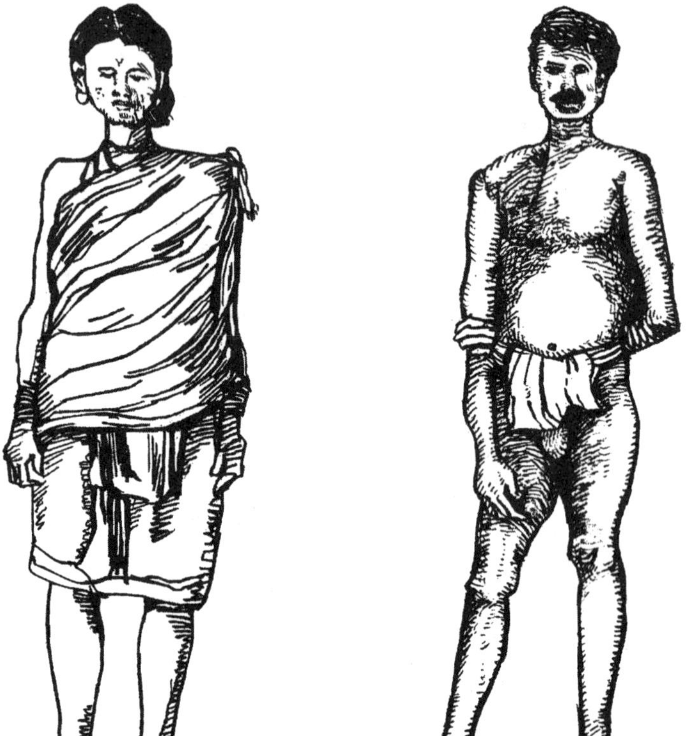

Hairstyle of Kutia Kondh Female.

Tattooing

The women have their arms tattooed with geometrical and floral designs. Older women who are skilled in this job are employed by younger women to give tattoo marks. Before a woman gets married she gets these tattoo marks on her body, the purpose being to beautify herself and not for anything else.

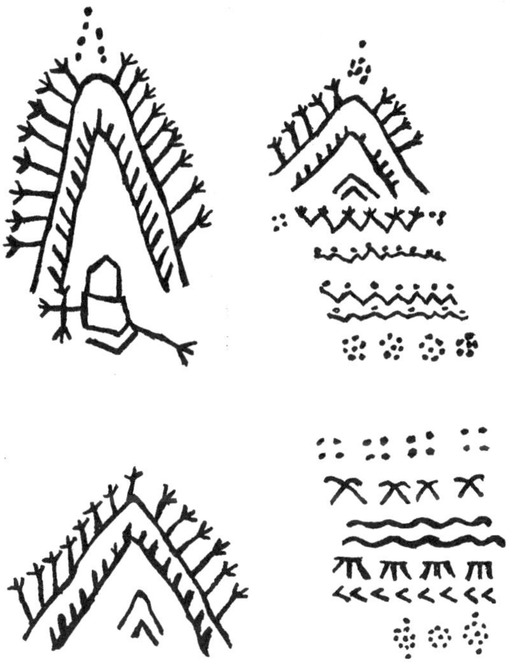

Ornaments

The Kutia Kondh women wear ornaments of various types. Some of them have gone out of use and some are still being used. A description of some typical ornaments is given below:

KAPA SIKIDING AND *KASADA MADA* (HAIR PINS)

Kapa sikiding and *kasada mada* (hair pins) are made of an alloy of iron and brass mixed together. These hair pins have gone out of use, but these are being preserved as valuable old ornaments.

Kasada Mada
(Hair pin)

Kapa Sikiding
(Hair pin)

KALU, KAJU, BINA AND *MUAN MUDI*
(FINGER, TOE, NOSE AND EARRINGS)

The women wear rings both in hand and leg fingers. The former are called *kaju mudi* and the latter *kalu mudi*. The rings are made of either silver or copper. Rings are also used for nose.

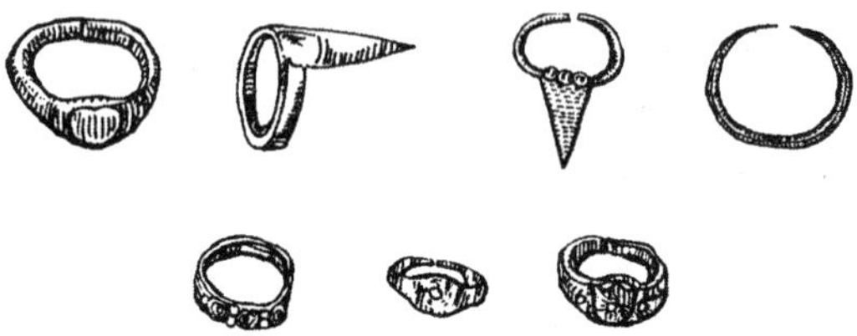

KIN KICHADI (EARRINGS)

The lowest ring of the ear lobes is made of gold while those used in the upper lobes are made of brass. In some cases more than a dozen such rings are found to have been used in each ear and as a woman grows older she uses more and more of such rings.

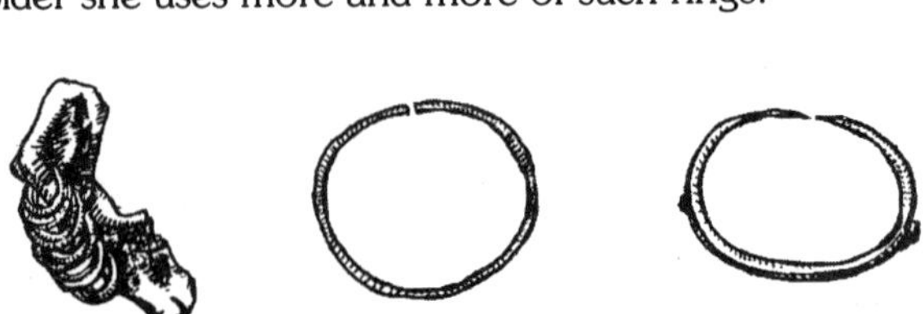

TODERI (WAIST BELT)

Both unmarried and married women are found wearing an ornament of the type of waist belt made of silver or alloy. Many women are found wearing four to five or more of such belts around the waist. One piece costs about Rs. 100. They get this ornament done by the goldsmiths at the time of their visit to the Kutia villages.

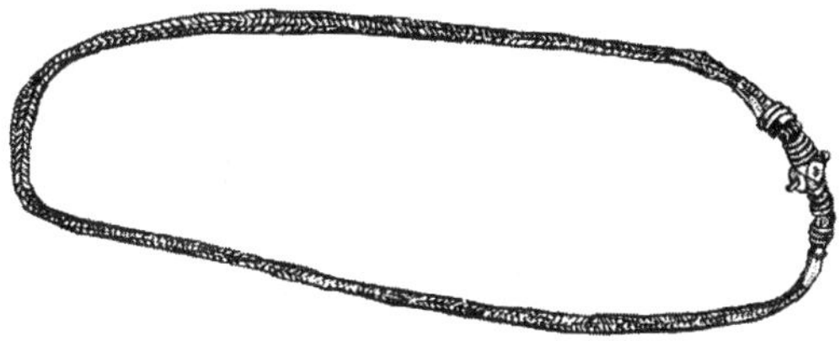

KAGDA (NECK ORNAMENTS)

The *kagda* is a rounded single piece with a hook at one end to be inserted into a socket at the other end. Women both young and old are found wearing such ornaments in large numbers around the neck.

Besides *Kagda* they use necklaces of beads and coins.

RASA PADANGI (BANGLES)

Bangles of various kinds made of glass or brass are a favourite of the Kutia women.

7

Musical Instruments

Muang Lauri (A Musical Instrument of Pellet-Bells or Hollow Rattle Type)

It consists of an iron rod bifurcated at one end, each piece holding sonorous hollow brass bodies containing a number of loose pellets which rattle when the rod is struck on the ground with the other end.

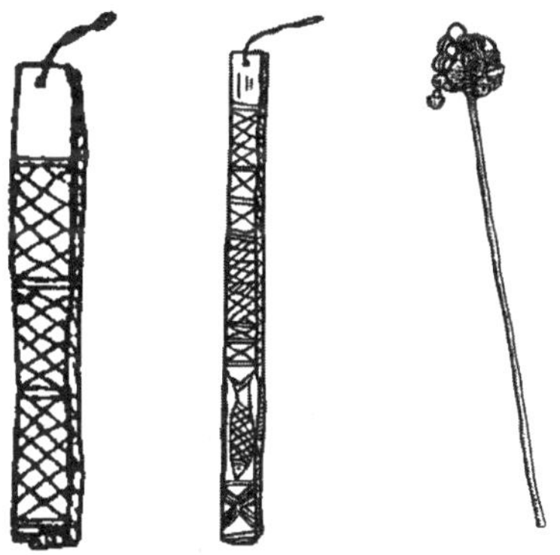

Basi (Flute)

It is made of bamboo. One end of it is closed by gum and the other end is provided with a narrow slit through which air from mouth is blown while playing. Four holes are made on the body for playing with fingers for producing different musical sounds.

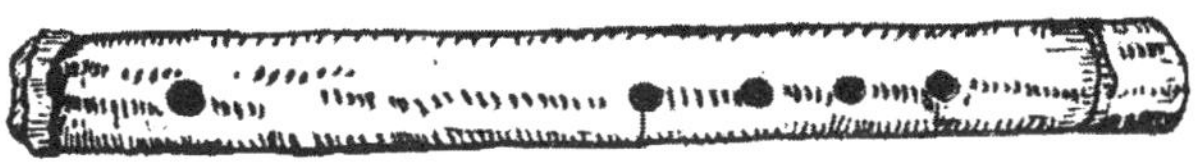

***Dadam* (Single Membrane Drum)**

A membrane of goat skin is stretched across the rim of a hollow drum made of damani wood. The drum is kept hanging from the left shoulder under the arm-pit and played by both hands by striking the membrane with bamboo sticks.

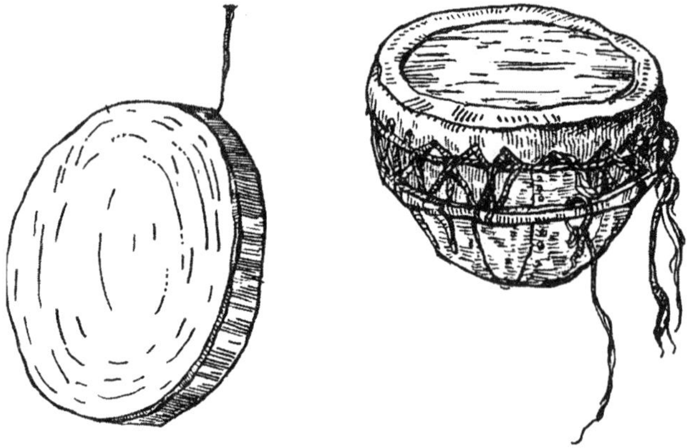

***Kabda Lauri* (Dried fruit with Seeds Inside making Sonorous or Rattle Sound)**

The plant locally called *kabda* yields long and thin fruits with seeds inside. During summer season when the fruits become dry these are collected and used as a musical object. When it is shaken the seeds rattle and produce a musical sound.

***Kama* (Aeolian Flute)**

The flute is made of buffalo horn with its natural hollowness. The horn is curved and one end is solid and narrow and the other end is open and wide. The solid portion is also made hollow. While playing a jet of air is blown through the opening at the narrow end to produce

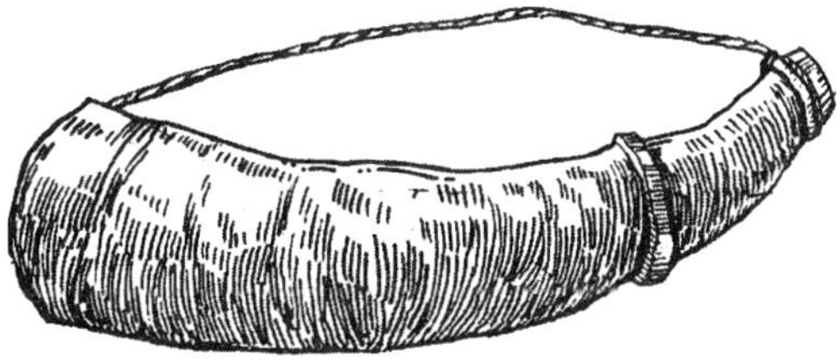

sound. The instrument is used in festivities, while welcoming guests at the time of marriage ceremonies. As the sound is produced louder than other instruments, it is used at night to scare away small animals while watching the crops in the swiddens.

Janging (Clapper)

Two circular clappers connected with a string are played by striking one with the other.

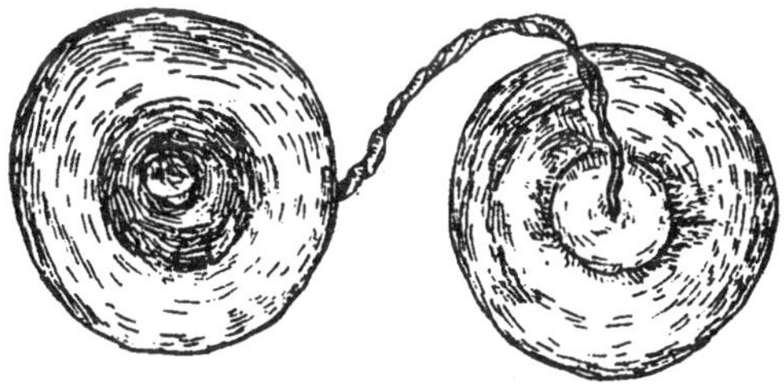

8

Religious Objects

Dharani Vali (Mother Goddess)

THE Mother Goddess is installed in the middle of the village street. The deity is represented by three pieces of stones kept within a bamboo enclosure. On festive occasions, the village *Jani* applies turmeric to these stones and offers rice whenever a buffalo or a poultry is sacrificed in the field. The bones of these animals are offered to the deity. During *Kedu* festival the buffalo is sacrificed in the field outside and the head of the sacrificial animal is offered to the deity.

Dehu Penu (Shrine at the Entrance of the Village)

This is also a village deity worshipped with *Dharani Vali*.

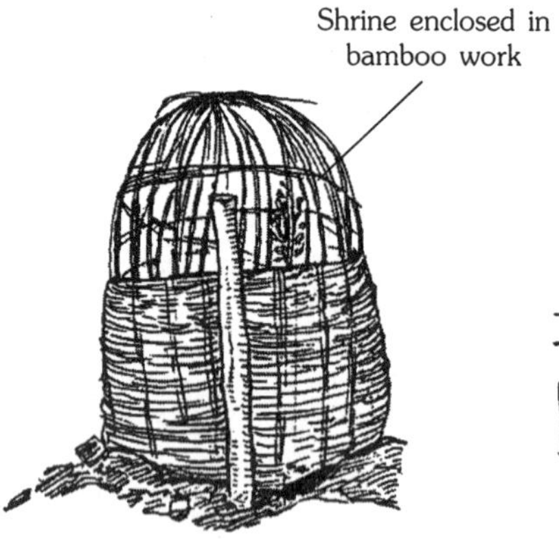

Dharani Vali

Shrine at the middle of the village.

Shrine at the entrance of the village.

Timba Dedi (Wooden Deity)

The wooden deity consists of a single piece of *sal* wood which is notched at its upper end and geometrical art forms are carved out on the outer surface. The base of the deity is left with a solid mass of wood to make it stand on the floor. A bell is hung at the upper end for ringing during worship. During festivities, the wooden deity is worshipped by the Jani in every house. The deity is placed adjoining the right side wall of the living room.

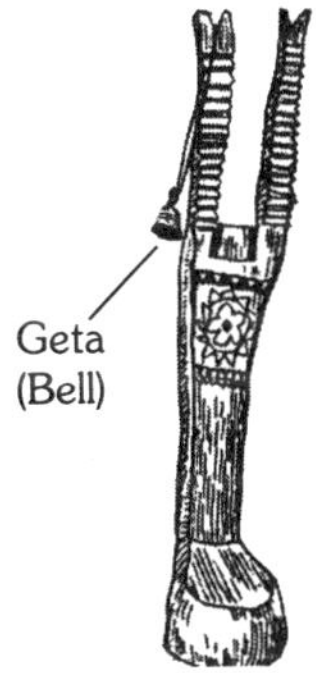

Korumunda (Sacrificial Post/Meria Pole)

This is a wooden post fixed on the ground in the street of every Kutia village. The wooden post is made of *sal* wood. Its upper half is divided into two parts to carve out designs of semi-circular types. It is made by communal effort and Kutia males are entrusted with the task. The buffalo to be sacrificed is tied to this pole, and the Kutias celebrating the occasion, hack the animal with their axes to death during *Meria* festival.

PART II

Dongaria Kondhs of Koraput and Kalahandi Districts

9

A Short Ethnographic Account of the Dongaria Kondhs

THE Dongaria Kondhs are found living in the Niyamgiri hill ranges which comprise four Community Development Blocks namely Bissamcuttack, Kalyansinghpur, Muniguda and Biswanathpur of Koraput District. The Dongarias stand separate from all other sections of the Kondh tribe for their skill in horticulture. They grow pineapple in vast stretches of land in the hill slopes. These pineapples are planted in places where the jackfruit trees are present so that the leaves of the jackfruit trees provide shade to the pineapple plants.

The Dongarias are also skilled in banana plantation in the hill slopes along with turmeric and ginger cultivation. Plenty of mango trees are found in the hill slopes which are under such plantations. Citrus plants such as orange and lemon are also grown in convenient places in the hill slopes along the streams flowing in the hills.

Side by side they also carry on shifting cultivation, but it is done in a limited manner restricting this cultivation to the hill top. They grow cereals like *ragi* and some minor millets which are their staple foods. Those who have plain lands in the valleys grow paddy which is used also as a food crop.

The Kondh is a major tribe of Orissa. Its population in the 1981 census was 9,89,342 which makes 17 per cent of the Scheduled Tribe population of Orissa. The Dongaria population would be around 6000 which makes roughly 0.70 per cent of the Kondh population.

Dress and Ornaments

A Dongaria male wears a cloth called *kodi* of sixteen feet in length and one foot in width. It is wrapped round the waist several times and then passed between the thighs so that one end hangs in front and the other end at the back. Some Dongarias use a shirt when they go out to the market. A woman uses two pieces of cloth called *kapda-ganda,* each of three feet in length and one-and-a-half feet in width. The first piece is wrapped round the waist with a knot in front. The second piece hangs around the waist and one end of it passes through the armpit and tied at the back to cover the upper part of the body. Both men and women cover the body by means of a piece of scarf with embroidery work on it.

Both males and females are fond of using ornaments, and sometimes it is difficult to differentiate the sex of a person from a distance. A wooden comb (*kakuya*) is fixed at the hair knot at the back by both sexes. A tiny knife (*pipli*) is used by the ladies at the hair-lock. Ear-rings and noserings are used by both the sexes. A knife and an axe are inseparable companions of a male. A tobacco-pipe either of bell-metal or wood is fixed at the waist so artistically by a man that it looks like a sort of ornament. The women use necklaces of beads and coins in bunches. On ceremonial occasions the women wear waist bands and more earrings to look attractive.

Food

The staple food of the Dongarias is *ragi* which is taken three times a day with rice, green leaves and vegetables. They are also fond of taking dried fish, chicken, mutton, buffalo flesh, pork and beef. Almost all ritual and festive occasions, when animals are sacrificed, are observed by taking animal flesh.

Roots of tubers and mushrooms collected from the forest are also eaten along with the staple food. The Dongarias are very much addicted to liquor. They savour *mahua* liquor and *sago* palm juice greatly. In addition to these liquors, mango liquor, jackfruit liquor, banana liquor, molasses liquor, etc. are brewed at home and taken on festive occasions. They also chew tobacco which they carry in tobacco containers wherever they go.

Social Organization

The family consisting of parents and unmarried children is the smallest social unit among the Dongaria Kondhs. Marriage is monogamous among them. Widow remarriage is permitted in their society. Extended families consisting of parents and their married sons are also met with but their number is much less as compared to nuclear families. The family is patrilineal, patrilocal and patriarchal. Arranged marriage is common but cases of marriage by capture and marriage by service are also met with. Sororate and levirate types of marriage are also prevalent among the Dongaria Kondhs.

Adasbetta (Spinsters' Dormitory)

Every Dongaria village has one or more spinsters' dormitories depending upon the number of spinsters present in the houses. The boys of other villages visit the girls at night and spend time in dancing, singing and merrymaking.

Socio-political Organization

Every Dongaria village has a political organization with village leaders and elders as members of this organization. The village priest called *Jani* is the religious head and also the formal head of the village council. All matters concerning the village are referred to him and he decides these matters either by himself or in consultation with the members of the council depending upon the nature of the matter. The post of *Jani* is hereditary. Next to *Jani* comes *Bisimajhi* who functions as an assistant to *Jani*. Whenever *Jani* is absent, he presides over the village council and adjudicates the cases in consultation with the other members of the council. The main duty of *Bisimajhi* is to collect revenue both from land and forest, from each household and function as the custodian of the fund. The village messenger known as *Barika* who is *Domb* by caste calls people to attend the village meeting whenever it is held.

There is another set of village leaders who are sacerdotal in character. *Pujari* is one of such functionaries who holds the umbrella made of bamboo during *Meria* festival. He is the man whose axe falls first on the animal during *Meria* sacrifice and then others follow suit.

Dehuri is the medicine-man who is skilled in occult practices and knowledgeable in folk medicine. *Bejuni* is the *shaman* who performs divination and brings supernatural beings under her control through recitation of incantations. Her services are sought to ward off evil spirits and sometimes cure illness by magical means.

Gouda and *Jhatuni*

They belong to Domb community. The former herds the cattle and takes them out to graze and brings them back to the village in the evening. The latter sweeps the village street and keeps it clean. Both of them serve as mediators in business transactions and the Dongarias are obliged to these servicemen for their help in sale and purchase of goods.

Every Dongaria village has a village council and the elders are members of this council. The *Jani* of the village convenes a meeting whenever needed and presides over it for adjudication of cases which are referred to the council by aggrieved parties. Cases such as quarrels between persons, breach of taboo, commitment of offences, partition of property and cases of inheritance, illegal love affairs, etc. are settled in the village council. Inter-village affairs are referred to the *Mutha* council. *Mutha* is an important socio-political organization. It comprises a group of adjoining villages. Some such *Muthas* are called *Jakasika Mutha*, *Wadaka Mutha*, *Pushika Mutha*, *Kadraka Mutha*, *Nishka Mutha,* etc. The entire Dongaria area is divided into 21 *Muthas*.

Each *Mutha* has a headman called *Mandal*. During feudal regime the *Mandal* used to serve the feudal lord in various ways and was honoured as the leader of the *Mutha* by the feudal chief on the occasion of *Dashahara* festival. A turban was tied by the feudal chief on the head of the *Mutha* as a mark of honour shown to him for his services to the chief. The inter *Mutha* affairs like boundary disputes, land disputes, bride-capture and bride price are settled by the concerned *Mutha* heads. A Dongaria of a particular *Mutha* cannot own land in any *Mutha* other than his own, nor can he participate in any festival which is observed at the *Mutha* level.

Religious Beliefs and Practices

The Dongarias believe in many gods and spirits. They worship them and offer food and drink on various festivals and ritual occasions. *Dharani Penu* (Earth Goddess) is their supreme goddess. She is installed in a hut in the village street. The hut is called *Kudi*. Next to *Dharani Penu* are many village gods which are propitiated on festive occasions. *Kateivali Penu* is installed by the side of *Dharani Penu*. Next comes *Jatrakudi Penu* which is installed in a hut at the outskirts of the village. Besides these gods and goddess, there are several other deities and spirits in and around the village. Most of these deities are malevolent and bent upon causing harm to men, animals, crops, etc. *Kudi* (*sadarghar*), *koteasal*, *jatrakudi*, *tulimunda* (middle post in the house), maidens' dormitory, *Bejuni*'s house, are considered most sacred. Of all rituals the *Kedu* festival (buffalo sacrifice) is most important. It was formerly called *Meria* festival when human beings were sacrificed. But after it was abolished during British regime it is substituted by buffalo sacrifice and therefore it is called *Kedu* (buffalo) festival. It is observed for eight days and *Dharani Penu* is worshipped on this occasion for a good harvest and for the prosperity of the people.

10

Human Habitation, Settlement Pattern and House Types

Forms of Dongaria Kondh Villages

THE Dongaria Kondhs have many distinctive features in their settlement pattern, house types, economic life, dress pattern, social organization, political system and religious beliefs and practices which stand them as a unique tribal group. The Dongaria village is situated wherever there is a shelf in the steep hills or in the gentle slope at the foothills. Every village has a long and wide street running in east-west direction. The houses are built close to one another on either side of the village street. In some villages there may be two or more such rows of houses existing at a little distance from the main street.

Everywhere the Dongaria Kondh villages sit in the east-west direction. There is a reason for such sitting. The Kondhs believe that the presence of their creator-sustainer deity symbolized by the sun is necessary at all times for their well-being and harmony in villages. The presence of sunlight can be maximized by setting the village street in the east-west direction. Moreover, this east-west setting of the rows which enforces north-south setting of each household ensures sharing of sunlight equally by all households.

There is another benefit of this east-west setting of the rows of houses. Such a setting has a warm side in winter and it is very pleasant to sit on this side and work. Also being set on a slope, the rain water drains out rapidly without flooding the houses and the village street is thus kept clean at all times. In other seasons, the heat of the sun dries the soil and removes dampness, a condition which favours a

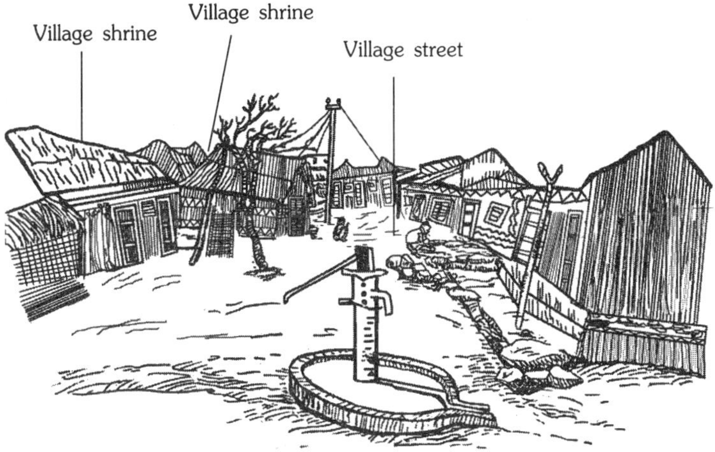

View of Khambesi village.

Backside view of Khambesi village.

comfortable living. At the outskirts of the village, by the side of the road leading to the village, is a shrine of the deity called *Jatra Kudi*. In the same place, there is present a small shed for the village Goddess called *Thakurani*. The village community hall-cum-shrine of *Jahir*, earth Goddess or *Sadar Kudi,* as it is called, is present in some places in the main street of the village. The girl's dormitory is always built at the back of any of the two rows of houses preferably close to the stream or river flowing nearby. There may be more than one dormitory depending upon the size of the village. There are hills on all sides of the villages with plantations of fruit-bearing trees in the hill slopes. Patches of shifting cultivation are also met with in the hill slopes preferably at higher altitudes.

Types of Dongaria Kondh Houses

Before taking up the construction of a house, the house owner performs certain divinations and rituals to test the suitability of the site for habitation. A Kondh house requires as many as 60 wooden pillars which are collected from the nearby forest. Before these posts are set in appropriate places, some geometric designs are carved on them not for the sake of any ritual considerations but as a matter of decoration.

Front side of a house.

First of all, two posts, one in the eastern side and the other on the western side, are fixed in the middle of the plot. These are the longest pillars of the house. Generally, they are each 13' 6" in length. Nearly 3' of the post remains buried in the pit and the remaining 10' 6" inches stand above the ground. A beam of 13' 6" is fixed on these two pillars.

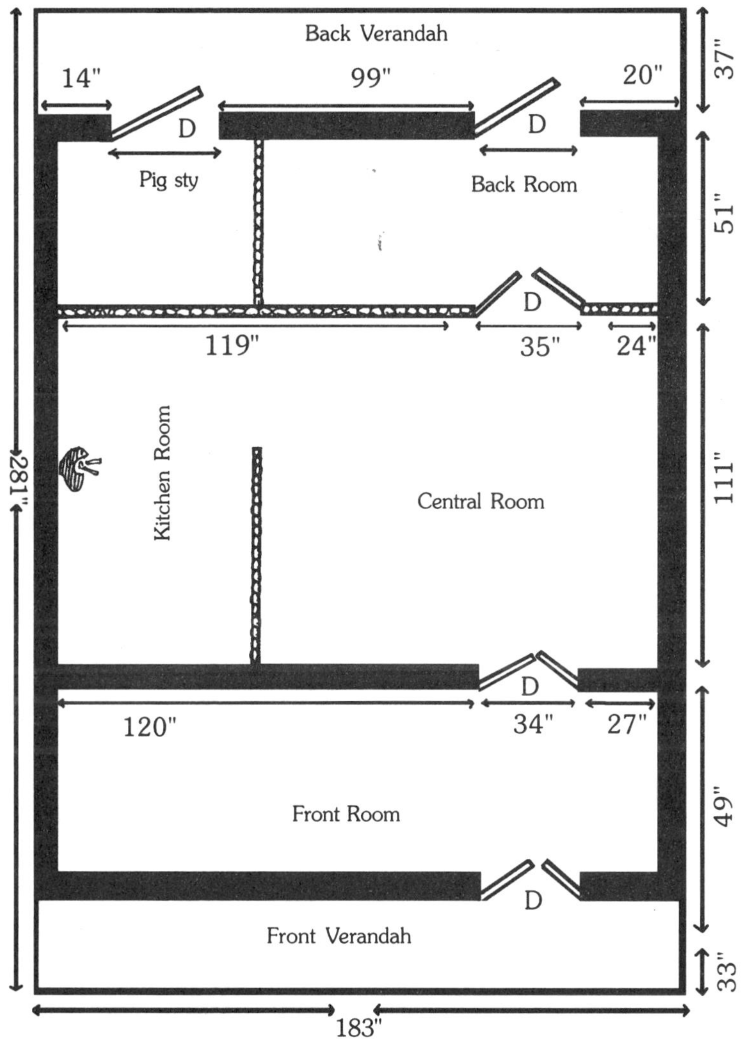

Ground plan of a house.

On the northern side and the southern side of these two tallest posts, 20 posts, 10 on each side, are fixed on the ground. It means that five posts in the east and five posts in the west on the northern side and similarly five posts in the east and five posts in the west on

Aka Giri (Backside view of a house).

Munda (Wooden Post)

Dhueri (Door).

the southern side are fixed along the line of the two central longest posts. These 10 posts on each side get shorter and shorter in height and a beam is fixed on each pair of these posts. Then five posts are fixed along the line which will form the back wall of the front room. One beam runs over the five posts. The height of these posts is equal to the height of an adult man. Likewise five posts are fixed along the line which will form the wall of the back room and a beam runs over the posts from side to side of the house.

From the front verandah six poles, three in front and three in the back are fixed on the ground. A beam is set on the three posts in front and another beam is set on the three posts at the back side. Likewise six posts are fixed in the back verandah, with two beams, one on three posts in front and the other on three posts at the back.

Inside the house four posts, two in the northern side and two in the southern side, are fixed and a beam is fixed on each pair of these posts. The purpose of putting the beam on these posts is to enable the rats to move along these beams. Similarly three posts are fixed in the back room and three in the front room, each supporting a beam along which rats move.

Dapa (Inside view of the Back Room).

Holu (Oven).

There is an inner chamber in the south-eastern corner of the central room. This chamber is situated in front of the hearth which is located in the south-western corner of the room. This inner house has three posts on the eastern side and three posts on the western side. The posts in the east support a beam and those of the west support another beam. The chamber has walls on three sides and is open on the hearth side.

Loft

The central room has an overhead loft. To support this loft, four posts — two on the southern side and two on the northern side — with supporting beams are fixed on the ground. The loft has an opening just above the hearth and a post with steps carved on it is fixed on the ground near the hearth. This post is used as a ladder to climb up onto the loft.

Another small loft is provided above the hearth. This is used for keeping foodstuffs on it. The overhead loft is used as a store for keeping agricultural and forest produce, clothes and ornaments and other household materials. The loft is set at such a low height that a man cannot stand erect in the room.

View of the loft.

Papi Munda.

The outer walls are made of wooden poles set close to one another on the ground and plastered with mud. The inner walls are made of sundried bricks plastered with mud.

The roof of the house is of gabled type in the sense that it slopes down on both sides from the ridge pole. The east-west setting of the rows of houses on either side of the village street makes every house sloped in the north-south direction. The rafters are of bamboos which are fixed to the beams starting from the ridge pole to the eaves of the house. Bamboo splits are laid over and under the rafters and tied at several places by means of siali fibres. Thus, the roof trellis steeply slope on both sides of the house. It is thatched with a kind of grass locally grown abundantly.

The Dongaria house has a verandah in front as well as at the back. The passage from the front verandah leads to the front room which opens to the central room by the eastern side of which is located a small chamber which serves as the abode of the house deity. The kitchen is in front of the house shrine. The central room leads to the back room, by the side of which on the eastern side, the pig sty is located. Both the back room and pig sty open in the back verandah. The oven in the kitchen is a two-in-one, fed by firewood through a single mouth. An earthen platform is made close to the wall in the kitchen room for keeping cooked food, cooking vessels and water pots.

The Dongaria house is built with a low roof-ridge with eaves coming down low over a high verandah. This makes entry into the house possible only by crouching. These architectural peculiarities are governed by the climatic condition of the locality. The low eaves prevent damage caused to the mud walls by the flashing of the rain water. Moreover, the warmth inside the house is maintained making indoor living comfortable in all seasons particularly in winter when the cold is severe in the area.

Wall Paintings

The Dongaria houses show typical wall paintings. Some of these wall paintings are shown in the following sketches.

Wall paintings in the living room.

Adisbeta (Spinsters' Dormitory)

Spinsters' dormitory is a single roomed house with walls on all sides. The ground plan is square in shape; having a small verandah in front. The house has a gabled roof and in most cases thatched with straw. The dormitory is provided with only one door in front. The walls are made of bricks, plastered with mud. In some cases, mud walls are used. A wooden stump (*munda*) is posted inside the room just near the door frame. The post is being used for locking the door by placing a wooden stick in-between the closed door and the post. The door is small and one has to crawl in order to enter the dormitory. The door is made of *bija* wood.

At one corner of the house the floor is lowered down. At another corner of the house, beside the doorway on the floor, an elevated rounded platform is made for keeping the pestles. At another extreme corner of the room two small wooden pillars are posted on the ground and a beam is placed over it horizontally for hanging clothes of the females. The fixture is also used for placing on it baskets (*matra*) containing grains.

The dormitory is constructed by communal effort. Both males and females of the village help in its construction. Young boys of two

Dasi Hada (Spinsters' dormitory).

or three neighbouring houses form a group and fetch bamboos, logs of wood and grass from the forest while the girls help in preparing the mud and lifting it to the construction site.

As the first step, digging earth up to one foot is done and foundation is laid by packing it with stones. The brick wall is plastered with mud. The wall has no ventilators or any opening, rendering the inside of the house pitch-dark. The roof structure is made of bamboos and thatched with grass. The floor of the house is applied with cow dung by the girls. This makes the walls and floors look very neat.

Adolescent girls of three or four households, numbering about five or six, normally possess one dormitory. The real activity starts here after 6 o'clock in the evening, when all the member girls gather here after taking food in their homes. Apart from sleeping here at night, they do the husking of grains in groups. They prefer to do the work while gossiping and exchanging friendly jokes. Old ladies also use the dormitory along with the girls.

The dormitory in a Dongaria village is usually present behind the rows of adjoining houses. It is one of the most widely prevalent youth organizations in the Dongaria society. The number of dormitories present in a village depends on the numerical strength of adolescent girls available in a village at a particular time. Some villages have got as many as eight dormitories. The village society is very liberal in allowing unmarried boys of other villages to mix with the girls within limits of social rules.

Kading Hada (Cowshed)

The cattle shed is built separately at the back of the house. A low wooden platform at a height of four feet above the ground is made and screened on all sides by means of plaited bamboo wicker work with the entrance facing the back side of the house. A sloping passage is provided for the cattle to enter the shed.

Kading Hada (Cowshed).

Kaska Kuda (Poultry Pen)

It is a rectangular enclosure with bamboo mats covered on all sides.

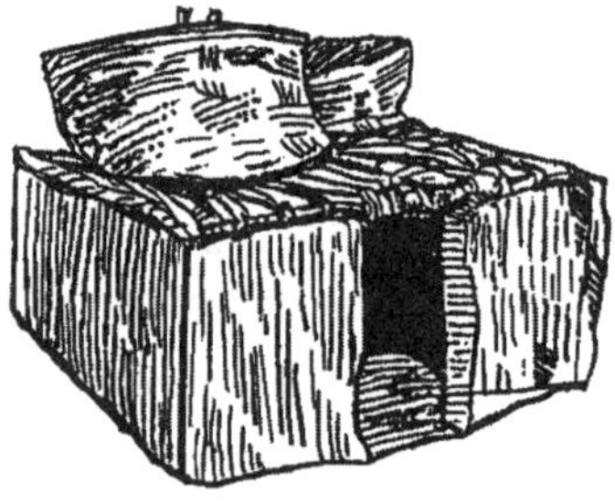

Kaska Kuda (Poultry Pen).

Pajing Kuda (Pig Sty)

The pig sty is provided at the back of the house. One part of the backroom is used by the women of the house and the other part is used as the pig sty which opens to the back side of the house.

Pajing Kuda (Pig sty)

Ada Hada (Goat Pen)

The goat pen is of the same type as of the poultry pen.

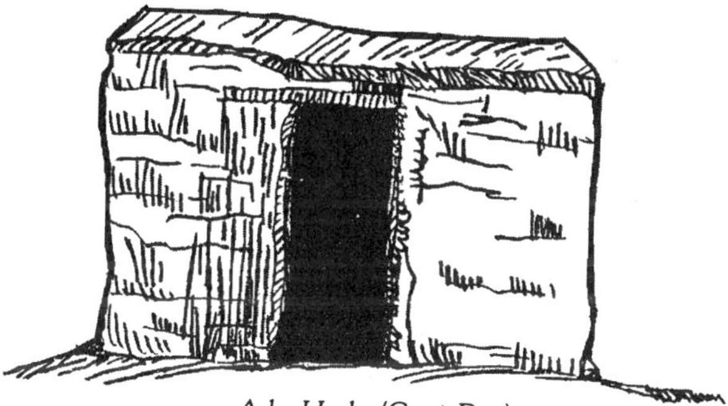

Ada Hada (Goat Pen)

Ladi Guda (Field hut)

A field hut is constructed in the field grown with crops or fruits. It is here a man sleeps at night to scare away the wild animals so that they do not destroy the crop. The hut has no wall on any side and has a slanting roof on wooden poles which rest on a tree on one end and one pole kept erect from the ground on the other.

Ladi Guda (Field hut)

11

Household Objects

Hatudi (Bamboo and Leaf Hat)

FLEXIBLE bamboo splits are used to weave the hat, inside of which *sal* leaves are fixed. It is made by the *Medra* community. Flexible bamboo-splits are woven in a criss-cross manner to have first two flat-pieces and then both joined in the form of a hat. The under surface is given a cover with sal leaves.

During rainy days a Dongaria puts on this hat and goes out to work in the field. As it is round and flat shaped, the entire body of the user is protected from getting drenched. As the hat requires great amount of skill and perfection in making, the Dongarias usually purchase it from the nearby market.

Ada (Measuring Brass Bowl)

Ada is one kind of measuring bowl.

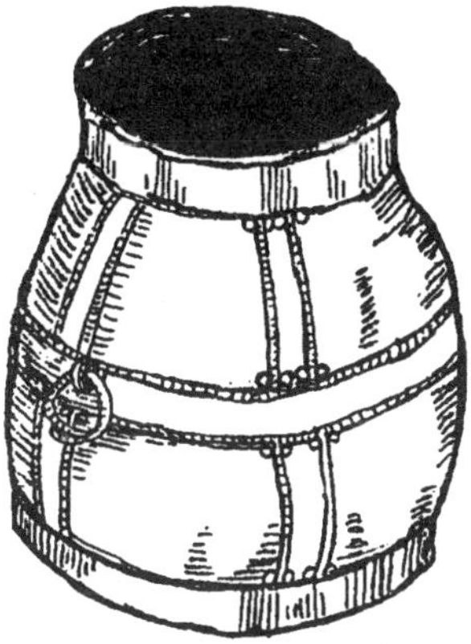

Manas (Measuring Wooden Bowl)

This measuring bowl is made from *sal* wood. The mouth of the container is given a covering with an iron ring around. The outer surface of the wooden bowl is semi-circular in shape with a flattened base. It is provided with a lid. Whenever anything is kept inside, its mouth is closed with the wooden lid. The wooden bowl is used for measuring different food grains, like *mandia*, *jhudunga*, *katunga*, etc. for exchanging these with other commodities whenever needed. The Dongarias are skilled in wood work and the *manas* presented here is one of their making. In olden times it was used in the barter exchange economy. Nowadays it is rarely in use.

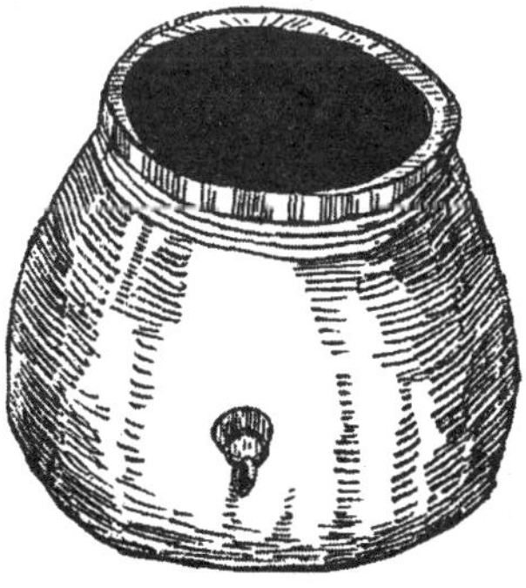

Jata Vali (Grinding Stone)

The appliance consists of two pieces of stone, semi-circular in shape, one piece placed over the other. Both the stones are uniformly thick. Two pieces of wood are also required to operate the quern. One wooden stump being smaller in size is called *kuti* while another wooden piece, shaped as 'L' helps in grinding. These wooden objects are

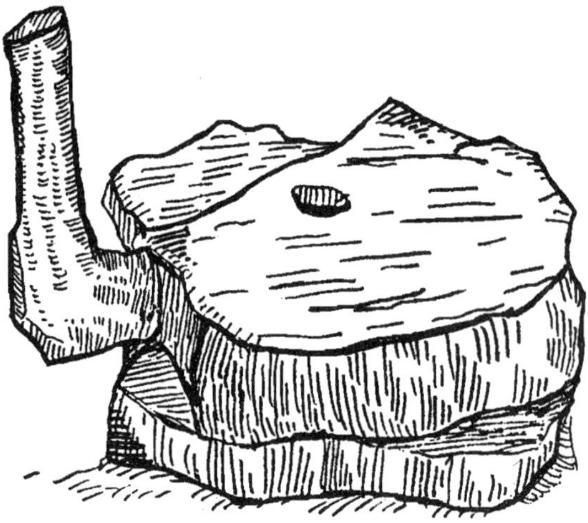

made of *hikeri* wood. After collecting the stone, the Dongaria trims its sides to give it a semi-circular shape. The bigger one is fixed horizontally, half buried in the ground. A tiny wooden stump is inserted tightly by boring the stone in the centre. Through the same process the smaller circular stone heavier in weight is worked. Then it is placed over the one which is fixed in the ground. The stump of the ground piece fits into the opening made in the centre of the upper piece. A hole is made in the side of the upper piece and the 'L' shaped peg is fitted into it. The Dongaria housewife, while busy in grinding *mandia*, *katinga* and *kandula* holds the 'L' shaped wooden stick in her right grip and moves the upper stone over the lower one in clockwise direction. Intermittently the grains are inserted through the bore at the centre. In this process the grains are ground into flour ready for cooking.

Dumuni (Serving Ladle)

The silver ladle has a long handle rounded in shape and a cup like structure at one end. It is used as a serving utensil for liquid substance. The cost of the ladle is Rs. 50. The silver ladle lasts for more than 10 years. It is rarely used in the present time. Nowadays some of the well-to-do families have preserved it as a show piece.

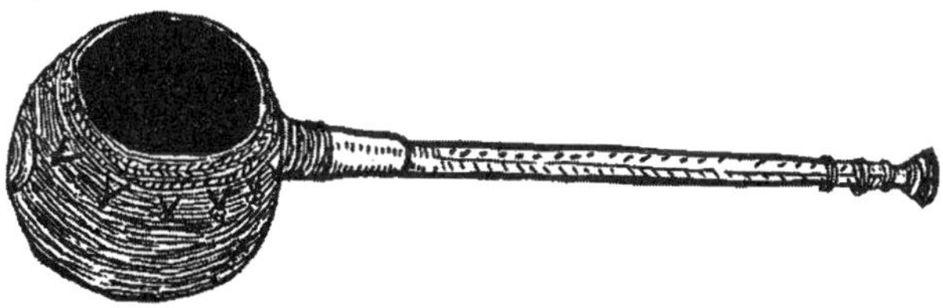

Dumuni (Gourd)

The object is a dried fruit having a hollow circular ring and a long stem attached to it, which serves as a handle for the user. To obtain a number of gourds the Dongarias sow seeds of *dumuni laha* under large trees in swidden fields. The seeds are dibbled in rainy season and in the month of December/January the full-grown gourds are plucked from the creepers. The gourds which are to be retained for use as ladles and containers are made to dry for a month or so. After the fruit is dried up, the upper portion is cut to have an opening and the inside is made clean. The shape and size of the opening varies keeping in view the use it will be put to.

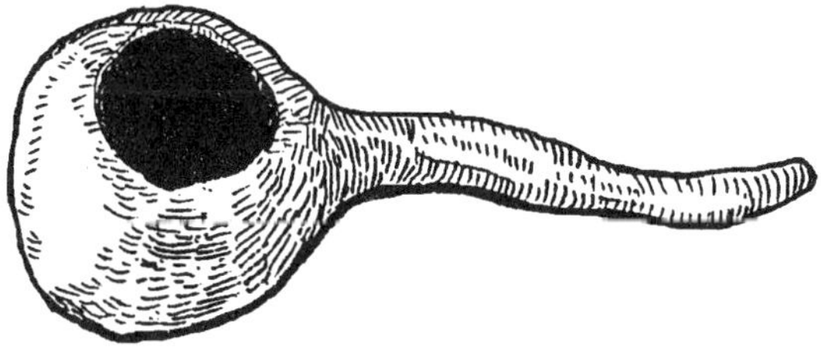

For serving drinking water and liquid substance the opening is made smaller and for serving rice the opening is made wide open. When it is used for storing seeds or for carrying goods to the fields, the long and narrow part is cut and removed. The Dongarias sell the gourds in the local market.

It lasts for three to four months according to the frequency of use. The gourd is also cooked with *dal* and potato and eaten. It is a matter of chance to distinguish between a sweet tasting gourd and a bitter tasting gourd as both are produced by the same plant.

Sunga (Tobacco Pipe)

The object is made of brass. Two pieces of hollow cyclindrical pipes are fixed together in which the upper piece is slightly curved. A tiny bamboo piece is attached by an iron chain to the lower piece at its end. It is made by the *Ghasi* caste. It is used by the Dongaria male for smoking tobacco. After filling the space in upper piece with tobacco, the user lights it with fire and the bamboo-pipe, that is, the lower piece is inserted at the butt end of the upper piece for smoking. The cost of the pipe is Rs. 10 and it is purchased from the market. It lasts for more than five years. It is rarely in use in the present society, so most of the males are nowadays habituated to chewing tobacco or smoking *bidi* available in the market.

Tobacco pipe used by men.

Sunga (Tobacco Pipe)

This tobacco pipe is made of brass. It has a bulbous hollow brass container with its mouth open. It is fitted to a small brass pipe through

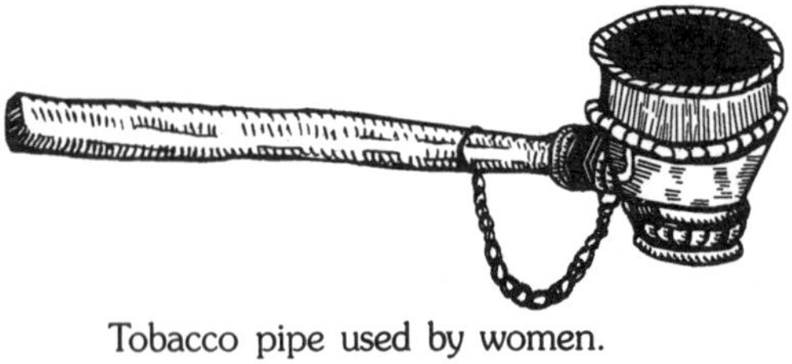

Tobacco pipe used by women.

which smoke is drawn into mouth. It is made by *Ghasi* caste. It is used by women for smoking tobacco. The hollow container is filled with tobacco leaves and fire is lit at the opening. The bamboo pipe is then inserted into the fixed brass pipe below for smoking. The cost of the object is Rs. 9. It lasts for more than five years. The pipe is mostly used by old ladies.

Madi Duna (Bamboo Container)

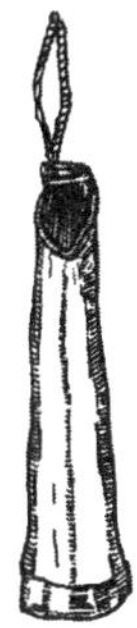

The object is a hollow bamboo piece having the natural internode at one end which serves as its base. The other end is kept open and wrapped round by a string for hanging purpose. Usually it is kept hanging from the wall or from the loft. The container is meant for keeping tiny objects like tobacco pipes, small ornaments, iron-nails, brass-made talismans, etc.

Mada Kalu (Beaker)

Mada kalu is made of gourd. A string is attached at its mouth to hang it on the wall. Water is carried in the beaker.

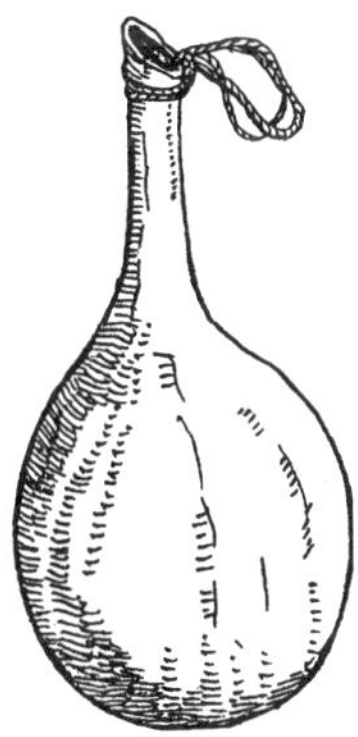

Kalu (Pestle)

It consists of a single piece of *damani* wood and a piece of iron ring fitted at the butt end of the pestle. A hole (*heni*) is made in the floor of the living room and the mortar is fitted into it. A single piece of *damani* timber is shaped into two parts. The lower shaft, which is longer than the upper half, is rounded and smoothened.

The upper part of the pestle is a solid and thick mass of wood intended for exerting heavy pressure on the grains while husking. This part of the club is hexagonally shaped. In some pestle one would come across geometrical art forms carved out at the joining of the two parts. At the bottom end of the club, an iron ring is inserted. While husking, the housewife, sits and stretches both her legs alongside the husking hole (*heni*) and puts the grains in the mortar using both her hands alternatively. Both the hands are also engaged alternatively for putting pressure on the grains. The husking holes (*heni*) are present in the living room (*eja*), in the back verandah (*dapa*), in spinsters' dormitory. Most of the women prefer to do the husking job in spinsters' dormitory in groups.

The husking job is usually done very early in the morning, in the afternoon, and at the dead of the night. Every female member, more than five years of age, does the work. Old ladies are not entrusted with the work as it involves hard and strenuous effort.

Takurani (Lamp Post)

It is a lamp with a decorative lamp post. It has also provision for hanging.

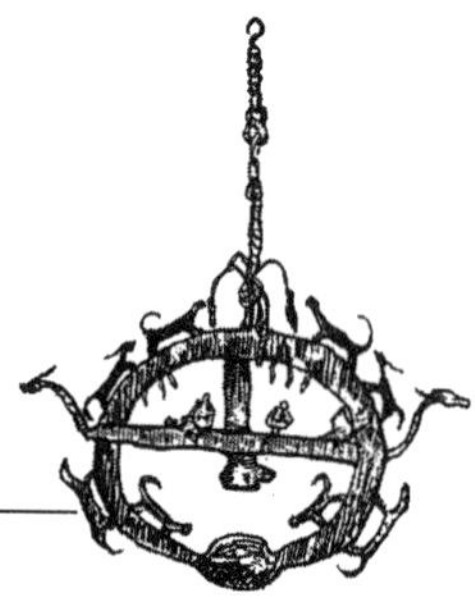

Pitda Dipi (Lamp)

The lamp is made of brass and fed with wick and filled in with kerosene. It is used in the living room.

Badti **(Lamp Stand)**

It is a lamp with a stand. It is made of brass. It is used in the shrine at home.

Dipi **(Lamp Stand)**

It is another kind of lamp fixed to a handle. It can be hung by means of the loop at the top of the handle.

Tatkadi **(Cowbell)**

The cowbell is a hollow piece of bamboo cut at one end in a U-shape form. A solid piece of wooden stick is suspended by its side. The cowbell is kept hanging in the neck of a cow. During its movement the wooden part strikes against the bell and makes sound. A missing cow is found out by the sound of the cowbell.

Suri (Knife)

The knife consists of a triangular-shaped pointed iron blade having a sharp edge and a tiny iron handle round in shape. Another accompaniment of the instrument is the case of the knife. The case consists of two triangular pieces of *sal* or *bija* wood scooped out inside and both the pieces are fixed by three iron rings. Thus, a case of wood is formed for keeping the knife in it when not in use. To make the instrument more decorative, a skin case is formed as a covering for the wooden case. The knife is used for cutting small plants, bushes, etc. Creepers are cut to prepare ropes. Goat's and

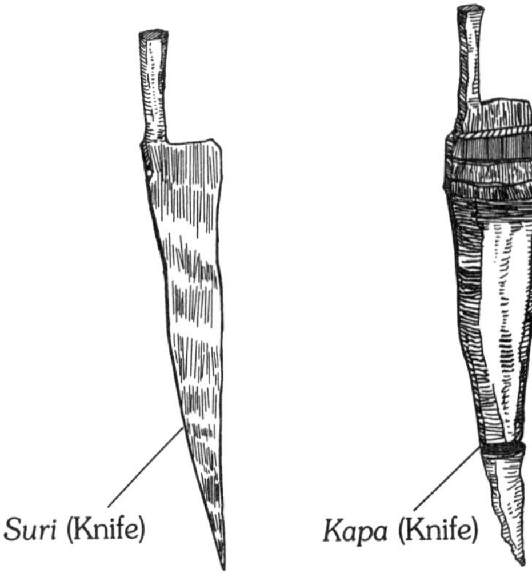

pig's flesh are also cut into pieces with the knife. The Dongarias carry it along with them to swidden fields. The knife along with the case is carried in the cloth wound around the waist.

The cost of the knife is Rs. 15 and purchased from the blacksmith. It lasts for years together. Nowadays, the knife is rarely in use though some of the old people have preserved the implement for fancy sake.

Khanda **(Sword)**

The sword consists of an iron blade slightly curved at the pointed end. The outer edge is sharp and designed for cutting. The other end of the blade is fastened with the hilt by an iron string and made to be inserted into the hilt. It is made by blacksmith. The sword has no practical use for the Dongarias. It is always kept over the partition wall in the living room. Only once in a year during the *Dashahara* festival it is brought out and worshipped before the goddess Durga. The sword costs Rs. 150 and is purchased from the blacksmith at the local market. The sword lasts for generations together.

Mudla **(A Wooden Hammer)**

The object consists of two pieces of wood. The handle is round in shape and is fitted to a mass of solid wood semi-rectangular in shape. Both the parts are made of *sal* (*sargi*) wood. In the solid mass of wood

a hole is made. A long wooden handle is inserted into the hole. During various festivals like *Meria Puja*, *Gantha Paraba* when the Dongarias organize grand feasts, the skulls of buffaloes are hammered down to pieces for the preparation of curry. After the feast is over, it is not used again and a new one is prepared before another feast is organized.

Pipel Katri **(Small Knife)**

The small knife consists of an iron blade attached to a tiny brass handle. The iron blade is sickle-like in shape. The blade is made by the blacksmith and the brass handle is made by someone of *Ghasi* caste. The Dongaria female uses the small knife while reaping crops like *Kusala, Mandia, Zhudanga*, etc. It is also used in digging out various roots from the forest and cutting ropes and creepers. Apart from its practical use, it has more of a decorative value. It adorns the hair of a Dongaria woman as she always tucks it in her hair lock. The cost of the iron blade is Rs. 3 while the cost of the brass handle is Rs. 4. The small knife lasts for more than two years.

12

Basketry

Unga Katra (Basket)

THE basket is wide open at the top and hung from the loft by a string tied to it. It is made as well as purchased by the Dongarias. The basket is made of flexible bamboo wicker work. The wefts pass under and over the warps singly and alternatively in diagonal direction. The rim of the basket is coiled basket work, as four numbers of wefts pass in front and behind each of the warps crossing them obliquely. Food grains and even meat are kept in it to dry. It is kept hanging from the loft by means of strings. It is also used as a carrying basket. Minor forest products are also collected and brought home in such baskets. The cost of a basket, if purchased from the market is Rs. 8. The basket lasts for more than two years. Owing to scarcity of bamboo in this region, most of the basketry are purchased from the market. But a few Dongarias are skilled in basket work.

Hanguni (Basket)

It is a kind of basket used for keeping vegetables and other things.

Watimuna (Pellet Bag)

Pellets are carried in this bag.

Banjeli (Basket)

The basket is provided with strings for hanging it from the loft.

Hitki

The basket is of the shape of a cap which is used for covering meat or fish while drying them in the sun so that the crows do not take them away.

13

Food Quest

Tahapa (Hoe)

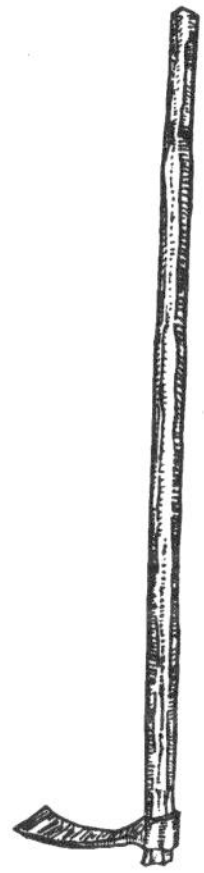

THE hoe consists of wooden handle made of *Damani* wood and an iron blade with a blunt edge. The wooden shaft is fitted into the socket of the blade. A tin packing is given in-between the joints to keep it intact. The hoe is specially prepared for hoeing the swidden fields and digging out weeds. The women use the hoe for all these works. But there is no taboo for men to use it. The cost of the iron blade is Rs. 10 at the market. It lasts for four to five years.

Gunch (Pellet Bow)

This is a minor hunting implement consisting of two parts — the bamboo stave and two strings. One end of the string is tied with the notch of the stave at one end and the other end having a loop is fixed to the notch of the stave at the other end. The strings when in use remains stretched in a straight line holding the stave in a bending position. The two strings are kept apart by means of a small piece of wood fixed in the middle and adjoining to

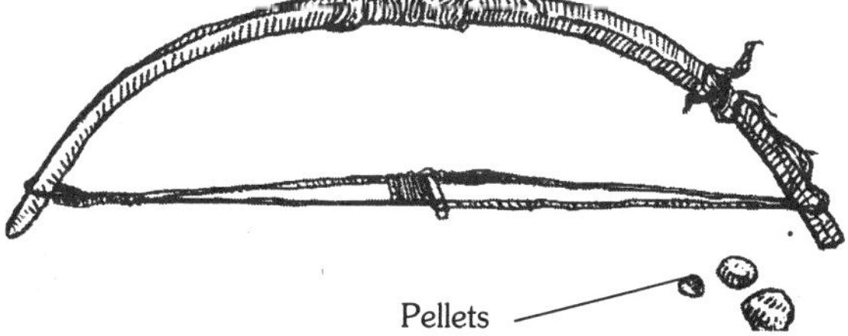

a pouch made of cotton threads. The pouch is meant for holding the clay-made pellets which are released aiming at the target. The stave is made from a piece of tough bamboo split. Both the ends of the stave are made pointed. At both the ends notches are made to hold the string. One end of the string is tied to the bottom notch permanently and the loop in the other end is fixed to the notch when in use.

The string is made out of a leaf of a wild plant. After the leaf is dried up, thread-like fibres of it are formed into the string and soaked with a gum collected from a wild tree. The pellet bow is used by the youngsters. It lasts for one year. When it is not in use, the bow is kept hanging from a nail fixed in the wall after loosening up the loop from the notch.

Ambu (Arrow)

The arrow consists of two parts. The shaft made of a light bamboo and the arrow head, a thin triangular piece of iron blade having sharp edges on both sides. The head is fixed at one end of the shaft and there is a notch, either single shouldered or double shouldered,

at the other end. At this end, feathers of hen are tied by means of cords of either skin or cotton. The arrow head is fixed to the shaft by inserting the pointed end into the opening made for this purpose and cords are wrapped tightly around the portion holding the arrowhead. The iron arrow head is made by the blacksmith.

Kolu Munda (Wooden Club)

The wooden club is made of a single piece of *Damani* wood. The shaft is in some cases hexagonally shaped and in others made rounded in shape. The carved head is pointed towards the end. The Dongaria culture is rich in wooden objects. The clubs of numberless varieties are a speciality of the Dongarias.

The wooden club is used for ceremonial purposes. Old people carry it along with them on their left shoulder. Apart from its ceremonial use it is also used as an offensive and a defensive weapon.

Welu (Bow)

The bow consists of two parts, viz. a bamboo stave (*welu*) and a bamboo string (*madiwacha*). The bow stave is an elastic piece of bamboo tapering at both ends. The stave has two notches at both its ends. The string loop is placed permanently at one notch and it is shifted to the other notch when in use and loosened when not in use. The shape of the stave is semi-circular. Bow string is made of bamboo split. The cord used for tying the bamboo string with the stave is made of fibres of sago palm tree.

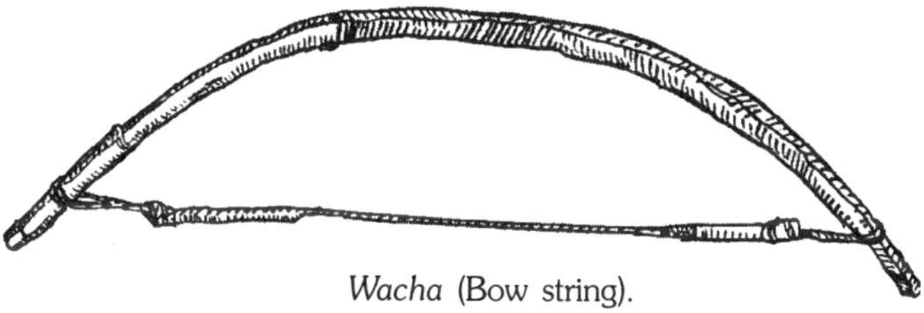

Wacha (Bow string).

Notches at both ends of the stave are carved out by knife. While using the weapon, the user usually holds it horizontally, holding the stave by the left grip. The arrow is usually discharged by fixing the arrow notch into the bow string. It lasts for a year or two. A bow is used in one hunting season and a new one is made for use in the next season.

Gajjeri (Spear)

The weapon has two parts consisting of a bamboo shaft and a triangular piece of iron-tipped blade. The iron-blade is purchased from the blacksmith. The triangular blade is inserted into the bamboo socket at one end, while the pointed end is directed upwards. The sides of the blade have sharp edges. At the base of the iron-head, two ring-

like structures are fixed to give it a decorative look. It is used as a piercing weapon thrown from a distance for killing poisonous snakes. The iron blade costs Rs. 10. It lasts for four years.

Kuta (Axe)

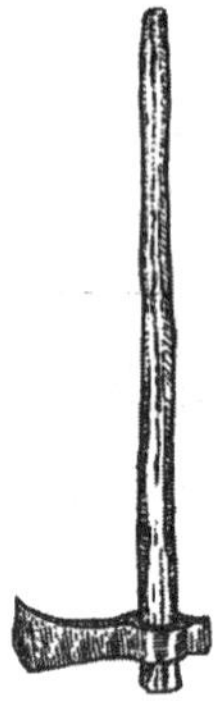

The axe consists of two parts — a rounded wooden shaft made from *damani* timber and an iron blade with a sharp convex cutting edge. The blade is fitted to the handle by means of the socket of the blade and kept tight by a tin packing inside the socket. The axe is used mainly at the time of hunting in summer days and also during ritual performances for sacrificial purposes. Only the iron blade is purchased from the local blacksmiths at a cost of Rs. 45.

Ichun Kdali/Mila Kdali (Small Axe)

The axe consists of a wooden shaft made of *damani* wood and an iron blade. The iron blade has a socket at one end to insert the wooden shaft. The wooden shaft is round in shape and smoothened by means of a specially made knife. The wooden shaft can be made by any Dongaria male. The iron blade is purchased from the market from the blacksmiths. After preparing the shaft or handle, it is fixed into the socket and a tin packing is given to hold the blade intact. The surface of the iron blade is engraved with various geometrical art forms by the blacksmith.

The small axe has various uses for a Dongaria. He always carries it along with him, resting the iron blade on his left shoulder and the shaft hanging at the back. Apart from its use for cutting trees and branches for firewood, he always carries it as a personal belonging. When he goes to his swidden field he clears his path by cutting down, with the axe, the creepers, thorny plants and branches which obstruct his way. The iron blade costs Rs. 15 at the market. The implement lasts for more than three years though the shaft is changed in five to six months. Every household has got more than one such small axe. It is also used in festivities when buffalo and goat are sacrificed.

Simne (A Typical Axe)

The axe has a handle (*deta*) and the iron blade. The handle is fixed to the socket of the blade. The outer edge of the iron blade is sharp and convex. At both ends of the sharp edge, two v-shaped depressions are made. The weapon comes to the use of the Dongaria male at the time of hunting in summer day festivities. Animals are sacrificed with this axe. Only the iron blade is purchased from the local blacksmith (muli) at the cost of Rs. 45. Nowadays, the axe is rarely in use as most of the offerings are made by using small axe.

Weg (Sickle)

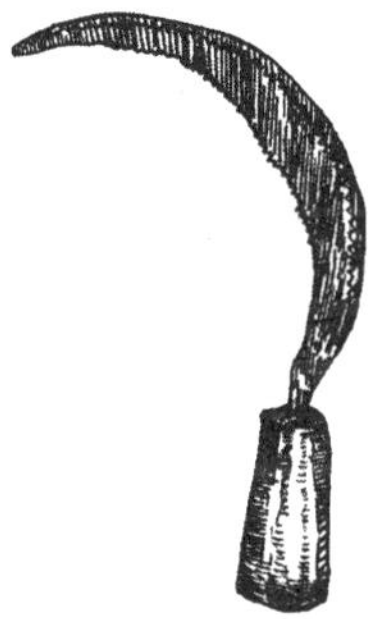

The sickle consists of a small wooden handle made of any timber like mango, *damani*, etc. and a curved iron blade pointed at one end with the arching edge teethed. The iron blade is made by the blacksmith and the wooden handle is prepared by Dongaria male. The blade part is fixed to the handle at one end. It is used for reaping various crops when they are ready for harvesting. The cost of the iron blade is Rs. 10. The durability of the implement is only two years after which the teeth get worn and edged out.

Kaja Kdali (Adze)

The adze consists of a wooden handle made of *damani* wood and an iron blade. The girth of the wooden shaft is more than that of the small axe. The shaft is round in shape. The iron blade has a socket into which the handle is fitted. At the other end, the adze has a blunt edge. The iron blade is purchased from the blacksmith. After preparing a round-shaped wooden shaft, the user inserts the head end of the shaft into the socket of the blade and a tin packing is given to hold the blade intact. The adze has the only use of cutting trees and splitting wood into small pieces which are used as fuel feeding the oven conveniently. The iron blade costs Rs. 25 at the market. The implement lasts for more than five years though the shaft is changed after five to six months. Every household has got more than one such adze.

Kuti Kera (Bamboo Stick)

The implement is a slender bamboo stick at one end of which there is a curved piece of branch of about 10" long. It is used for spreading the paddy plants over the threshing floor and collecting together the straws after the crop is threshed.

Mlallu Duka (Rabbits' Trap)

A few loops are kept hanging from a string, one end of which is tied to a bush and the other end to another bush. The string is kept straight and tightly tied to the bushes so that the loops are kept hanging. When a rabbit tries to pass by it is caught by the loops.

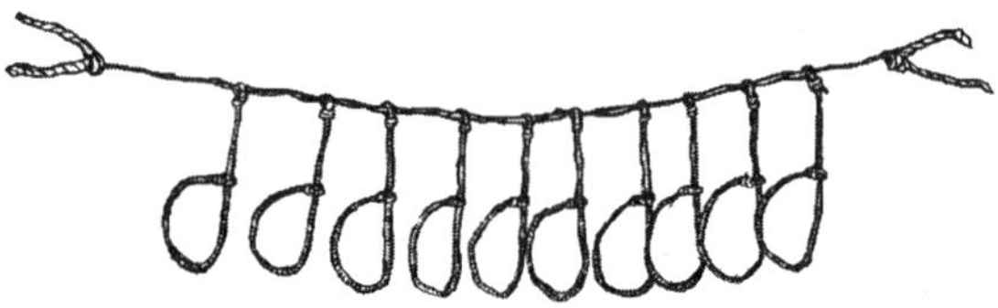

Guruti (Bird's Cage)

This cage is used to keep birds which are caught from the forest.

14

Personal Care, Dress and Adornments

Dress of Men and Women and their Hair Style

THE dress of men and women has been described in the ethnographic account of the Dongaria Kondhs.

Figure of a Dongaria woman (*Palang Wadka*).

Portrait of a Dongaria Woman (*Pule Wadka*).

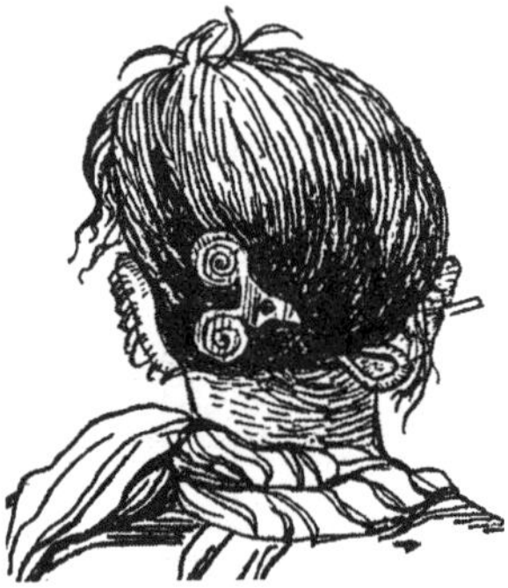

Hairpin in the hair lock.

Scarf

The scarf beautifully embroidered by the Dongaria girls is a specialty of the Dongarias. Both men and women cover the upper part of their body with scarves. A woman gives presents of scarf to her lover and they do not part with this scarf.

Embroidery on a scarf.

Kakawa (Comb Made of Buffalo Horn)

As the comb is prepared by the Dongaria male himself, a specially made knife (*kakawa katri*) and a wooden stump (*kakawa badga*) is required in its making. The comb is made of a small piece of buffalo horn having numerous teeth (*Palka*) on both the edges. The specially made knife has a small wooden handle attached with a tin blade having a wavy edge. The wooden stump is split into two parts at the top to hold the piece of horn in tight grip during its making. As a first step the horn is soaked in water for a couple of days. After the horn

Kakawa (Comb made of buffalo horn).

absorbs sufficient water it becomes soft and easier to work with the knife. Thereafter the horn is cut into small pieces. A small piece of horn is inserted into the split gap of the wooden stump, one edge of the horn standing out. It facilitates the maker to make the teeth of the comb. The Dongarias, both male and female, are fond of using combs which are fixed to the hair as an item of decoration.

Sipna (Hairpin)

It looks like a scissor having silver blades fastened at the middle. At the head end, two silver strings are coiled round to form two rings. It is made by the *Ghasis* as well as blacksmiths. It is pinned to hairlock from the side. It is used mostly by old ladies and sometimes by married women.

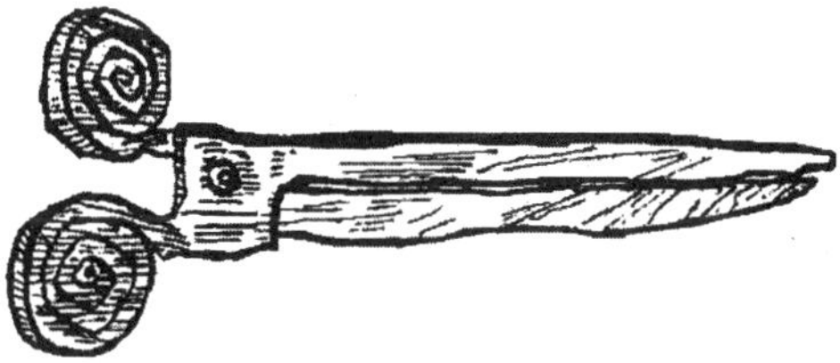

Kilamodi (Hairpin)

The ornament is made of a single piece of silver wire bent to make it 'U' shaped. This hairpin is made by the *Ghasi* caste. It is pinned in the hairlock along with the scissor like hairpin. The cost of the hairpin is Rs. 4.

Kagudi (Necklace)

Both iron and silver are used for making necklaces. The shape of the ornament is more or less circular. The hook at one end is fitted to the ring when it is used. It is made both by the blacksmiths and *Ghasis*. It is a common ornament used by Dongaria women. As many as eight to twelve such necklaces are found to have been worn in some cases.

Kagudi (Neckband)

Ahera (Necklace)

Daura (Talisman)

The object is a curved piece of brass, pointed at one end, having a small cavity to contain the roots of wild plants given by the magician. Three pairs of hooks are fixed on the upper surface of it to tie it around the neck by means of a string.

It is made by the *Ghasi* caste. The cavity contains medicines prepared from roots of wild plants given by the magician. It is usually worn by male children as Dongarias believe that fever and other diseases caused by evil spirits will not attack the child. A thread is inserted into the perforated hook for hanging it around the neck or tying it around the arm. The container costs according to its size and varies between Rs. 15 to Rs. 20. The medicine given by *disari* is available free of cost. It lasts for years together. Except Mondays and Thursdays, other days are regarded as auspicious for wearing the talisman.

Tadwa **(Armlet)**

This is a brass ornament, with flattened surface, circular in shape. The flat surface is engraved with several designs. The ornament is worn in the arm and kept tight by pressing both the ends together. The cost of the ornament is Rs. 20. It is specially used by newly-married women. The ornament is brought along with her from her parent's house during her marriage. When the ornament does not fit the arm it is used in the wrist.

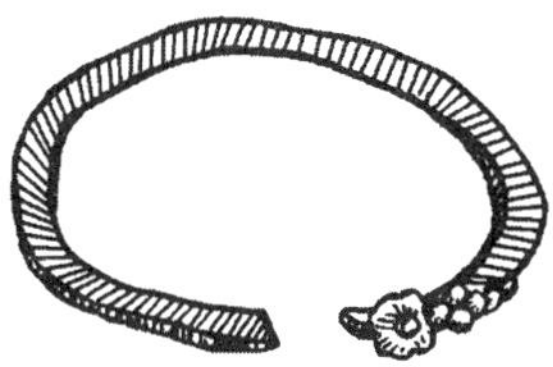

Kwte **(Earpin)**

This is a brass ornament having two small pointed parts, one part having a small hole and the other having one small knob fixed to it. The earpin is made by the *Ghasi*. The cost of the earpin is Rs. 2.

Nanguli
(Earring)

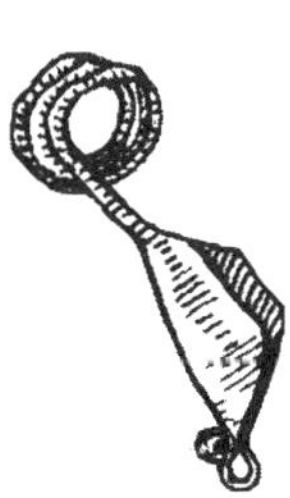

Nanguli
(Earring)

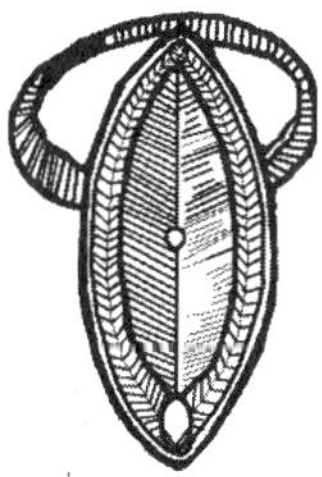

Sringi Sapa
(Finger Ring)

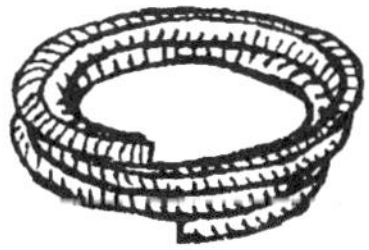

Mudi
(Finger Ring)

Anta Suta (Waist Band)

Both unmarried and married women are found wearing a type of waist band made of silver or alloy. Many women are found wearing four to five or more of such belts around the waist. They get this ornament done by the goldsmiths at the time of their visit to the Dongaria villages.

Kudi Linga (Tattooing)

Both men and women do tattooing on their body. Some of the below tattoo marks are shown in the sketch.

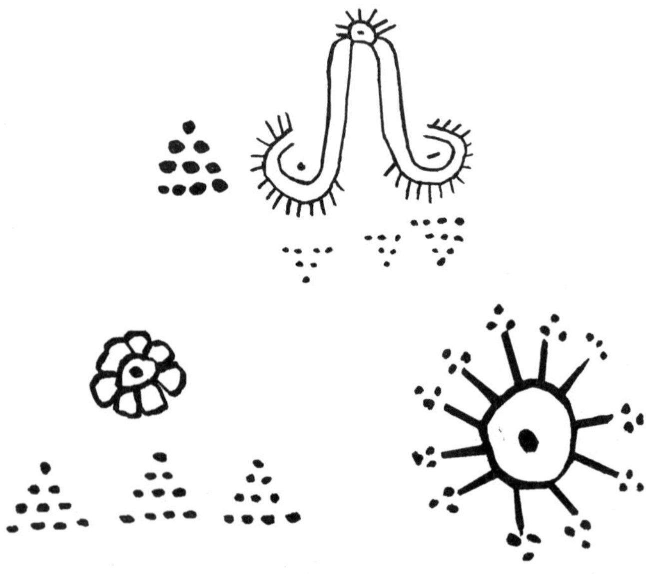

Kudi Linga
(Tattooing designs)

15

Musical Instruments

Dappu (Single Membrane Drum)

THE musical instruments consist of two parts one of which is the rim of wood across which a piece of goat's skin is stretched tightly. The rim of wood consists of pieces of curve-shaped wood of equal length, breadth and thickness and fixed with each other by small iron plates and nails. It is purchased from the local carpenters. The goat's skin is stretched round the rim. The drum sticks are made of bamboo. Two sticks are required for playing the drum which is hung from the left shoulder by means of a string made of *siali* creeper.

Dappu
(Single Membrane Drum)

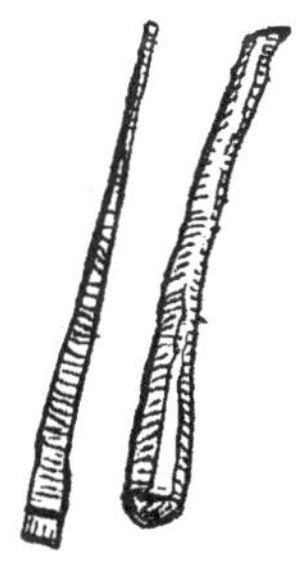

Dalanga
(Drum Stick)

The rim is purchased from the local market and costs Rs. 80 and the skin costs of Rs. 25. The instrument in most cases belongs to the community and is played on occasion of *puja* in association with other drums and musical instruments. Three to four such instruments are played at a time.

Nisheni (Single Membrane Drum)

The single membrane drum consists of a hollow iron base and the membrane is made from cow's hide. Two drum sticks are also prepared from the hard skin of buffalo. The iron base is made by the blacksmith and sold to the Dongarias. The hollow body of the iron base has a thick iron rod around the outer surface in the middle which is fixed by welding. The cow's hide is stretched across the mouth of the hollow body. The membrane is kept tight by tying it with the iron rod by means of strings made of the same cow's hide. The stretched membrane consists of two layers of hide. A circular piece is cut in the middle of the outer layer of the hide.

The instrument while playing is hung from the neck by means of a rope made of *siali* creeper and rests on the belly of the player. Both the hands are used to beat the drum by means of two drum sticks. The iron base is purchased at a cost of Rs. 400 from the market. The drum lasts generations together. When the instrument is purchased from the market a ritual is performed by the *Beju* inside the house before its use. During individual as well as communal festivals like *Gantha puja*, *Meria* festivals, etc. this instrument is used. A great amount of energy is required to hold the heavy drum and stand erect for playing hours together. Cow's hide nowadays is a scarce item, and it is difficult to replace an old drum with a new one.

Janjinga (Clapper Series)

This musical instrument consists of two specially shaped identical pieces of wood. Two openings are made in each piece. Both the openings towards the end are fitted loosely with iron rings by means of a nail. These rings clash with each other and produce sound when shaken. Usually adolescent girls play this musical instrument when they dance in a group when the male visitors of their age come from other villages to spend the night with them. The young girls dance with them in some isolated places. While dancing they sing songs and play with

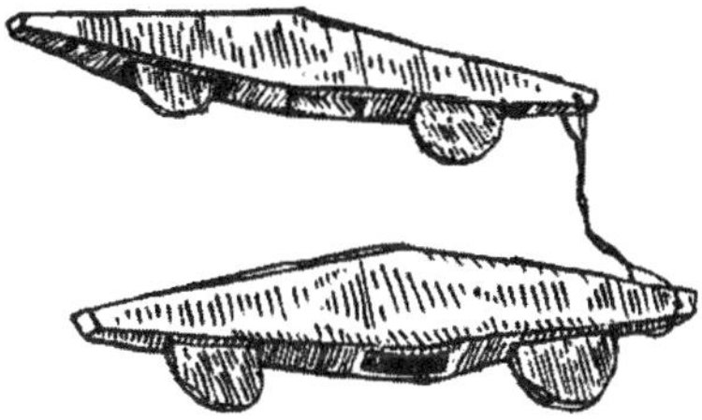

clappers for music. These clappers are kept in the spinsters' dormitories.

Gininga (Cymbals)

The Dongarias use cymbals while dancing. A cymbal is tied to each end of a string.

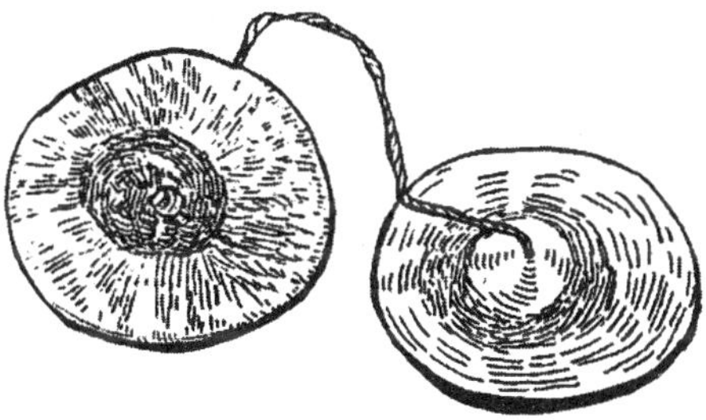

Surudi (Flute)

The flute is a cylindrical bamboo piece closed at one end and open at the other end. At the closed end a hole is made in the bamboo piece by inserting a hot iron rod. At the other open end of the tube a series of holes (about five in number) are made in a line through the same process. The young Dongaria boys are found playing the flute watching the crops alone in the swiddens.

16

Religious Objects

Gorada (Shrine)

It consists of three pieces of small carved wooden stumps and two long pieces of wood all stuck to the ground together.

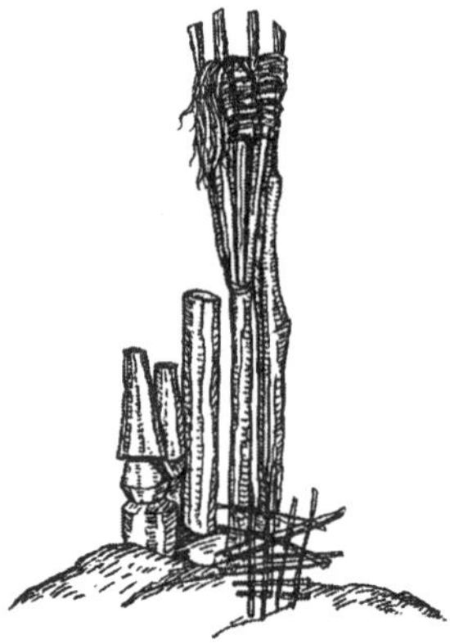

Jatra Kudi (Shrine)

The shrine of the goddess watching the village is located at the entrance to the village. The *Jatra Kudi* comprises wooden stumps arranged on wooden pillars which help the deity to rest above the ground.

Jatra Kudi
(Shrine at the entrance of the village).

***Kudi* (Shrine)**

The *Gorada* stumps which are stuck to the ground and kept erect are lodged in the *Kudi*.

Ber Penu

This shows the inside view of the shrine with a thatched structure under which the objects of worship are displayed.

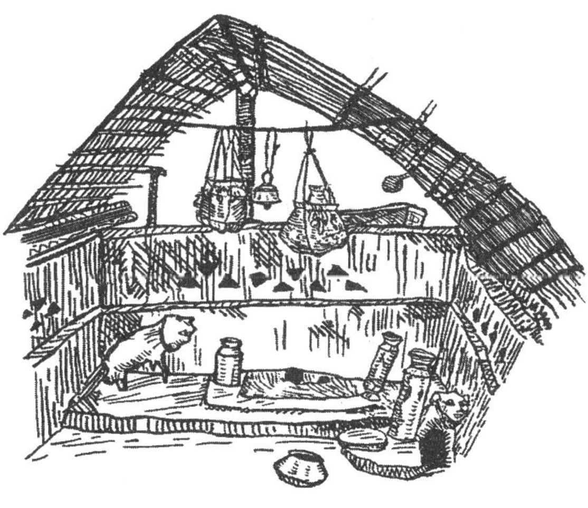

Father *Penu Jakir Kudi*

The wall paintings inside the shrine are shown in this sketch.

Ghata Penu Kudi

This sketch gives a view of the shrine.

Kateivali (Sacrificial Post)

The sketch shows the post where the animals are sacrificed.

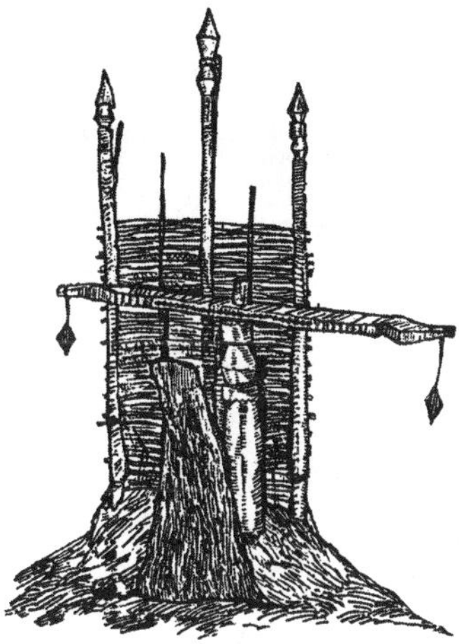

Paniki Munda

Kolu Munda (Ceremonial Club)

The club which is used for the ceremonial purposes is shown in the sketch.

Simini (Hatchet)

This axe is used for sacrificing the animals at the shrine.

PART III

Malia Kondhs of Phulbani District

17

A Short Ethnographic Account of the Malia Kondhs

OF the five sub-groups of the Kondh tribe, the Malia Kondh is one. They live in villages which are scattered throughout Phulbani district and some portion of Gajapati district. They speak *Kui* language which is a part of the Dravidian stock. The Malia Kondh villages are situated mostly in forest regions with hills of various heights and with very little plain lands. Some areas of these hilly regions are very difficult to access and are influenced by cultural contact with the non-tribal neighbours who are mostly Oriyas.

Settlement Pattern and Housetypes

A Malia Kondh village has an east-west setting with a common village street running in east-west direction. The houses of individual families are built detached from one another on either side of the village street facing each other. This linear pattern of the Malia settlement has many advantages. A *Meria* post and the shrines of *Dharani Penu* are located in convenient places in the village street. One of the houses represents the dormitory for the unmarried girls of the village. Some *Domb* houses are also located in some convenient places in the village away from the Kondh houses. At the outskirts of the village is a place where the sacred grove is located. At a distance from the village the cremation ground finds its place near the scrub jungle close to the hills. Every village has a common grazing ground where the cattle are let loose to graze. There may be cultivated fields where crops are grown. There are some plain lands which are reclaimed for paddy cultivation.

It is a rule that every Malia Kondh village is situated near a spring where people take bath and use its water for drinking. There may be also wells in some villages. Every Malia village must have a footpath which connects the village with the main road running at a distance from it. There may be one or two grocery shops opened by someone of the village or an outsider belonging to some other caste. There may be some government institutions such as a primary school or a small health centre in the village. Originally every village was homogeneous in the sense that it was occupied by people of a single clan. Now the villages have become heterogeneous in both caste and clan composition.

A Malia Kondh house is built on a rectangular ground plan. The house has a door in front facing the village street. A mud packed verandah runs in front of the house up to the main door. The next portion of the front part lies under the over-hanging eaves of the roof.

At the back of the house, the pig sty is provided. It opens to the back side of the house. A door is provided at the back of the house. On one side of this door, lies the pig sty and on the other side there is a small room used by women to stay during their menstruation period. By the side of this room, there is a space for fowlpen and goat pen.

The main room of the house is divided into different parts which are used for different purposes. On the left side of the central main room, the kitchen is present. There may be one or two ovens and a narrow earthen platform which is used for storing pots. The ancestors are worshipped in the portion set apart from the kitchen, and the sacrificial post is located in this portion. Outside the kitchen portion attached to the partition wall, a place is set apart to store paddy bins.

On the right side of the main room lies the cattleshed. This portion is separated from the remaining portion of the main room by a line of wooden posts stuck into the ground preventing the cattle to get into the central living room. By the side of the wooden partition is the hearth which provides warmth to the living room. This hearth is provided in a low earthen platform.

The walls of the house are made of either wooden planks or mud depending upon the availability of wood in the locality. The house is provided with a two sloped gabled roof thatched either by mud tiles or thatching grass.

Dress and Ornaments

There is nothing special to mention about the dress and ornaments of the Malia Kondh. They wear the same types of clothes and use the same types of ornaments as the neighbouring Oriyas do. But there is one speciality in their adornment which distinguishes them from other communities. The Malia Kondh women wear tattoo marks of various designs on their faces and these tattoo marks identify them as the women belonging to the Malia community.

Territorial and Political Organization

The largest territorial unit is called a *Mutha*. A *Mutha* may consist of 10 to 12 villages and each *Mutha* has a distinct boundary and a name. Formerly a *Mutha* had a headman called *Sardar* and to assist him in discharging his duties there were some assistants or *Paiks*.

The *Mutha* was an administrative unit inhabited by the Kondhs in large majority and there were also a few families belonging to Oriya castes and scheduled castes. The name of a *Mutha* coincides with the clan of the Kondhs and therefore the *Mutha* is taken as a clan territory. Previously a clan territory was homogeneous in the sense that the Kondhs of a single clan were living in a particular clan territory.

But nowadays the clan territory has become heterogeneous. The alien elements or the people of other clans coming from other clan territories have no right over the land of the *Mutha* to which they have migrated nor do they have any right to worship the *Dharani Penu* (Earth Goddess) of the *Mutha*. Similarly any type of ritual pollution of the original Kondhs (*Jombo Tana*) does not affect the Alien Kondhs (*Koda Tana*). Every *Mutha* has a headman called *Sardar*. The headmen at the village level are under his control. The functions of a village headman are as follows:

1. The village headman presides over the village council.
2. He takes care of the guests visiting his village.
3. He is very mindful that the festivals and rituals, which are observed at the village level for the whole community are held without any deviation either in time or in performance.
4. He negotiates with the headmen of other villages when any occasion arises.
5. He looks after the officials visiting his villages on occasions.
6. The post of the headman is hereditary. After his death a suitable successor in his family may be selected and appointed upon approval of the village council.

JANI

The priest or *Jani* is the chief religious figure in a Kondh village. His function is to celebrate the community sacrifices of greatest importance. He has assistants to help him in his duties. His office is inherited down the male line. The priest diagnoses by trance the source of any trouble or sickness which has affected the village. The Kondhs are most knowledgeable in regard to herbal medicines which they apply at the time of need. But they are not averse to modern medicines which are also used among the Kondhs.

DHARANI WORSHIPPER

The *Dharani* worshipper is the keeper or custodian of the *Dharani Penu*. He performs necessary rituals and offers sacrifices at the central *Dharani Penu* which is represented by some pieces of stone slabs installed in the village street. *Dharani* is believed to be the guardian deity of the village. The *Dharani* keeper is selected by the deity herself and the people accept him to function in this capacity.

Heads of Households

The head of each family worships the ancestors and other deities residing in the house and officiates at all ritual observances held at the family level.

Every Kondh village has a traditional village council consisting of village headman, village priest and the elder members of the individual houses. Except the Kondhs of the village no non-tribal is entitled to become a member of the village council. The meeting place is close to the headman's verandah. The meeting usually takes place in the evening, when the people return to their respective houses after their day's toil in the field. The village council is considered traditionally as the supreme authority within the village. The matters which are generally discussed in the village council are related to village common fund and setting of dates on which feasts, festivals and sacrifices are to be observed. The village council also deliberates about the communal hunt and matters concerning land disputes, settlement of interpersonal conflicts, witchcraft and cases of divorce.

It is believed that the ancestors and other deities are keen to know about the decisions taken by the village council. This is to ensure that truth and justice are followed in deciding the matters concerning the village life.

One important function of the village council is to allocate the hill plots among the villagers as per the needs and requirements of every household. As it is believed that the deities are also very particular to know as to how the village fund is utilized by the Kondhs, in every decision taken by the village council it is the aim of the members to see that truth and justice prevail.

Youth Dormitory System

The Malia Kondhs had a strong dormitory system but it is now under disintegration. According to the traditional Malia system they need to build female dormitories only. The young men belonging to other villages visit the girls at the dormitory at night. Sometimes both the young men and women dance together to the beat of drums. Chitchatting, singing and dancing are the regular features in the dormitory.

Social Organization

FAMILY

Family is the smallest social unit. Generally most of the families are of simple or nuclear type. It comprises parents and their unmarried children. It is the practice among the Malia Kondhs, like among other types of Kondhs, that as soon as a boy gets married he builds a house of his own and lives with his wife and children separately from his parents.

LINEAGE

The next bigger unit is the lineage which comprises a number of remembered blood related families. The members of a lineage live together in different hamlets of a village or in a group of villages. Many consanguinal families constitute together an exogamous division which is called '*Klambu*'. The members of a *Klambu* claim descent from common ancestors and occupy a distinct territory called *Mutha*. In this sense *Klambu* may correspond to a clan while *Mutha* a clan territory.

TRIBE

The largest unit is the Kondh tribe which is rather a *de jure* unit. The Kondh as a tribe has its own identity which is maintained by them at all costs.

Life-Cycle

BIRTH

A pregnant woman has to observe many taboos and restrictions for her own and the child's well-being. Some of these restrictions are that she should not cross a hill stream with running water and should never go anywhere near a cremation ground. She should not go to forest by herself alone because it is believed that the spirits may cause harm to her. She also observes some food taboos.

Delivery takes place in the back room of the house and the mother is considered impure for a number of days. The placenta is buried outside at the back of the house. The mother bathes the infant with warm water, massages it with oil and warm it by sitting near the fire. The mother is prohibited to take any sweet food. Certain specified tubers, roots and green leaves are restricted for her.

Insanitary living conditions unhygienic practices, and malnutrition are the main causes of infant mortality among the Kondhs.

DEATH

The Kondhs cremate the dead bodies. In the case of a natural death mourning, pollution and funeral rites are observed for a week. No food is prepared for three days in the bereaved household. It is being supplied by the neighbours. On the third day after the death of the person the purification rituals are observed. The families related to the bereaved household throw out their polluted cooking pots at the cremation ground and offer seed grains to assist the ancestor in carrying out farming as usual. There-after they start searching for a spider at the pyre. The spider is tenderly carried home and released in the living room. This process indicates that the Kondhs believe in soul which is represented in the form of a spider which stands for the deceased's spirits which is brought home to live with other ancestors.

The rituals and customs observed on the occasion of a death are an expensive affair. The Kondhs have to borrow money from others to meet the expenses of feasts arranged for the relatives and observances of many rituals.

MARRIAGE

The Kondh marriage is of two types, namely arranged marriage, and marriage by bride capture.

Arranged Marriage

1st Step

The groom's family visits the bride's house with a basket full of rice. If this rice is accepted by the bride's family it signifies agreement of the bride's family for this marriage.

2nd Step

The groom's father with other members visit the bride's house to fix the date for marriage. They go with some liquor which is called "agreement liquor."

3rd Step

The groom's party gives Rs. 300 to Rs. 400 in cash, a buffalo, some clothes, brass vessels and an axe to the bride's father on this occasion.

4th Step

Non-vegetarian feast takes place at bride's home before she leaves her parent's house. Upon arrival of the bride, a similar non-vegetarian feast is arranged at the groom's house. Liquor is exchanged at the third visit which ratifies the marriage agreement, and the feasts are symbolic of the approval of this marriage by the two village communities.

Marriage by Bride Capture

As in the case of arranged marriage, the marriage by bride capture undergoes several steps.

1st Step

The groom's young friends find a chance to capture the bride. After the bride is captured, the friends are entertained with liquor and food.

2nd Step

The girl's father visits the groom's house with village representatives.

3rd Step

The village council levies a fine of Rs. 300 in cash and a buffalo.

4th Step

The captured bride is brought back to her father's house and later she is taken back to the boy's village. The marriage by capture takes a little time to perform but at a lesser cost.

Religious Beliefs and Practices

Gods and goddesses of the Malia Kondhs are described below:

THE DHARANI PENU

The *Dharani Penu* is believed to be the great creator-sustainer deity. It protects the community and ensures fertility of crops, domestic animals and all Kondh households. It is represented by a heap of stones which are placed in the centre of the village or piled against the *Dharani* keeper's house. The hut which is built for her installation is called *Kudi*. There are also small heaps of stones at either end of the village street. She is called *Tana* (Earth) or *Tari Penu*. Though the *Dharani Penu* represents the union of both female and male aspects, the *Kotebali,* another deity, is believed to be a male deity and the *Dharani Penu*'s husband.

THE JAKIRI PENU

The *Jakiri Penu* is believed to be a male deity dwelling in his sacred shed, the Sadar. The *Jakiri* stands for the rising sun and is believed to be the first ancestor.

VILLAGE BOUNDARIES DEITY

The boundary deity resides at the outskirts of the village. The boundary deity forms an invisible barrier around the village so that no outsider can enter the village without propitiating him. The deity safeguards the village against the entry of hostile spirits and keeps them at bay. Among the Malia Kondhs the place of his residence is unknown to the people, but everybody thinks that he is present in some place in the main approach road.

HILL GODS

There are many hill gods residing in different hills and particularly in places located close to the hill-plots which are under shifting cultivation.

GOD OF HUNTING AND RAIN GOD

The god of hunting has lost his importance since the practice of hunting is in the process of decline. The rain god maintains the respect and reverence shown to him by the people.

Ancestral Spirits

There is a sacred place inside every traditional Malia house, where the family ancestors live. They are believed to be deeply concerned about the welfare of their descendants and the villages to which they belong.

The Malias perform certain rites and rituals to appease the supernatural forces. Animals such as buffalo, cow, pig, goat are sacrificed. In order to perform these rituals, there are special functionaries in each village. These ritual specialists are as follows:

JANI

Jani is the ritual head of the village. His post is hereditary. He officiates all village rituals and is given a special share of sacrificial animals.

PUJARI

The *pujari* presides over the *Meria* festival along with *Jani*. He prepares the bamboo umbrella which he dangles to ward off the evil eyes of the evil spirits. Previously the Kondhs used to sacrifice human beings on this occasion. That is why the festival was called *Meria*. But during the British time, the human sacrifice was abolished and in its place a buffalo is sacrificed and that is why it is now called *Kedu* festival.

The Malia Kondhs perform many rituals on various occasions. A list of such rituals is given below:

1. *Kedu* festival observed on the occasion of offering buffalo sacrifice to *Dharani Penu*.

2. Shifting village to a new site.
3. Constructing and installation of new *Dharani*.
4. Setting up ancestor shrine in new home.
5. Sickness rituals.
6. Witchcraft removals.
7. Birth and death rituals.
8. Paddy grain forming ritual.
9. Hill lentil ritual.
10. Harvest ritual.
11. Threshing floor ritual.
12. Clan gods' rituals.

Besides these and many other minor celebrations, the Malias practise magic, witchcraft and sorcery, whenever required.

18

Human Habitation, Settlement Pattern and House Types

Forms of Malia Kondh Village

THE villages inhabited by Malia Kondhs in Baliguda area do not conform to any of the patterns of Kutia Kondh or Dongaria Kondh villages. The Malia Kondh villages are set up in the plains having vast agricultural fields in and around the villages where they practise wet cultivation. The houses in a village are scattered throughout with large patches of land adjoining the homesteads in which vegetables, turmeric, mulberry for rearing silk-worm are grown. Mango and date palm trees are also seen in those lands.

Though the houses are identical in regard to the design and building materials used for construction, they face in almost every direction. The village has a number of lanes and by-lanes, straight and curved, crossing each other and footpaths approaching each and every isolated homestead. One would also come across mango groves as well as *mahua* trees bordering the villages. Cremation grounds are also found to be situated in one of these groves adjoining the village. Small open spaces are left in front of the houses facing each other for various purposes like meeting of guests during marriage, playing area for children and a place to entertain guests and outsiders during festivals and ceremonies. This open space is commonly used by closely situated households. The villages are exclusively inhabited by Malia Kondhs unlike other Kondhs who live along with *Panas* as their neighbours in the same village.

View of Sirubali village.

House Types

ASSOCIATED RITUALS

Before selecting a place for construction of the house, the male elders of the household go to the proposed site at night. They carry along with them some rice, *mahua* liquor (*arki*) and a few cups made of *siali* leaves. At the site, they keep those leaf-cups containing a few grains of rice in each and pour the liquor on the rice. These are offerings meant for their ancestors. After the ritual is over, they themselves enjoy the surplus liquor and return home. Next morning they again visit the same site to verify whether the grains are disturbed or not. The disorder of grains signifies the presence of some evil spirit in the site and therefore it is an unsuitable place for construction of houses. If the grains are found to be in the same order as they were left in the previous night then it is regarded as a symbol of sanction by the ancestors to construct the houses.

GROUND PLAN OF THE HOUSE

The ground plan of a Malia Kondh house is rectangular in shape. The walls on all sides of the house are raised from bottom to top by fixing wooden planks close to each other. The door in front and that at the back which are provided in the longer sides, correspond to each other. Coming out of the house through the back door, the vast backyard falls where the houseowner grows maize, mustard, tobacco plants, gourd, pumpkins and other vegetables.

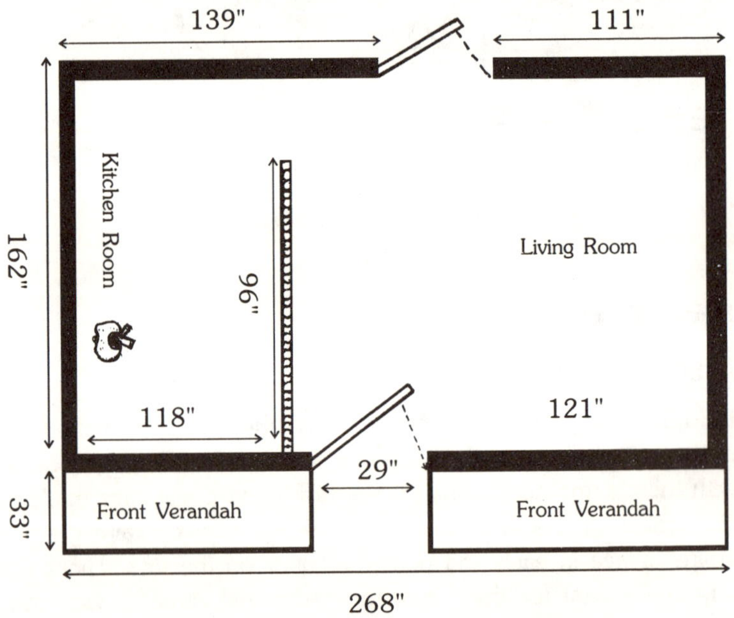

Ground Plan of a Malia Kondh house.

In a Malia Kondh house the floor of the house is raised above the ground level. Steps are provided to enter the house from outside. A verandah is provided in front of the house. A carved wooden post (*sahada kaba*) is planted in some convenient place in the house. It is used as a sacrificial post for offerings minor animals like goats, fowls, etc. on ritual occasions observed at home.

View of a Malia Kondh house.

View of a Malia Kondh tiled house.

Entering the house through the main door one would approach the main living room (*ija*). The main living room is divided into two portions. The smaller portion is occupied by the kitchen (*kadangija*), which is separated from the other portion of the room by a wall (*kadang kudi*) made of wooden planks arranged side by side from the floor level up to the loft level. The hearth (*solu*) in the kitchen is kept towards the extreme left corner of the kitchen adjoining one of the walls of the house. A small narrow passage is provided to enter the kitchen from the living room.

Inside view of the Malia Kondh Kitchen.

A loft is made above the hearth and this is used for drying boiled paddy grains before husking. The heat emanating from the hearth helps in drying the grains. Towards the right corner of the kitchen, the floor is used for keeping cooking vessels made of brass, silver, larger and smaller earthen pots for storing drinking water, etc.

The larger portion of the house is used as the main living room. In this portion one or two mortar holes for husking are embedded on the ground. This room is quite spacious in a few households. In others, the room is occupied by wooden shelves at one side and large grain bins placed on a wooden platform on the other side. Mostly these shelves are used for keeping baskets containing food grains like rice, paddy, turmeric, etc. for future requirements. This portion is also provided with a hearth for keeping the room warm in winter days.

The loft (*daadi*) overhead is made in the main living portion of the house. The loft is used for keeping various agricultural implements like axe, sickle, knife, pottery, country-made brooms and various other objects of the household.

The loft overhead is constructed by laying down three horizontal bars (*dula*) on both walls of the house crossing over the breadth of the house. Over it, wooden planks are arranged close to each other. The wooden bars are inserted at the ends into holes made in the walls for this purpose. The loft overhead remains at a comfortable height above the head spreading all over the main living room. A small opening is left near the front doorway to approach the loft. For approaching the loft, wooden ladders are used and in a few households the user approaches the loft by climbing through the front door which is just below the loft's opening. The valuable belongings particularly the ornaments and jewellery of the housewife is kept over the loft in a secluded corner.

LAUSKA (SPINSTERS' DORMITORY)

The most widely prevalent youth organization, that is, dormitory life in Kondh society is very rarely seen in Malia Kondh villages. Though some of the houses serve as spinsters' dormitory, which is a single room complex adjoining the main house, it is poorly maintained and in some cases in dilapidated condition. A hearth is also provided in the dormitory for keeping the mosquitoes away at night by burning cowdung cakes. The hearth is also used for boiling turmeric in large quantity after the harvest.

Dangadi Ija (Spinsters' dormitory).

GAHELI (COWSHED)

Individual households have cowsheds of their own adjoining the houses. The roof of the cowshed is straw thatched and it is very dirty inside the shed.

PATA (DOORS)

The doors at the entrance and exit of the house and the kitchen door are made of *sal* wood. The entrance door of the house is generally carved with different artistic designs on its outer surface for a decorative look. This door is generally purchased from the carpenter in the neighbourhood. All other doors of the house are made by the Malia male himself. The doors are single panelled and fixed to the door frames with two or three hinges. Both outside and inside, the entrance door is provided with chains, locks and latches.

To start with the construction of a house, a rectangular piece of land is cleared up. More earth is laid on the selected site to raise the floor level above the ground. At four corners of the plot, wooden pillars of *sal* wood are planted. All the pillars are buried up to three feet below the ground. For door frames, two pillars each of the same size and height are posted close to each other keeping in line with the other two posts each at the corner. The corner posts are called *nachakoba* and the posts meant for door frames are called *korvbanga*.

Before erecting the posts, grooves are made on two sides of each post facing each other. The wooden planks (*pangedka*) are arranged one upon another, side by side, from bottom to top. Both ends of the wooden planks are set into the grooves. Thus, the walls (*kudu*) of all the four sides of the house are raised. The narrow gaps in-between the planks are closed by applying red earth. To make the walls stronger, thick wooden beams, one from the inner side and another from the outer side are fixed together by inserting two to three wooden pegs. While these vertical beams at the middle of each side walls are called *tabedra,* the pegs holding them straight and tight from both the sides are called *kuti*. The side surfaces of the beams are barbed to give a decorative look to the house from outside.

The side walls (*talikudu*) are raised up to the ridge pole because of the gabled form of the roof. The planks that are arranged above the corner poles up to the ridge pole are kept intact by wooden beams (*tabedi*) fixed together by pegs from outer and inner sides of the walls.

ROOF STRUCTURE

The roof of the Malia Kondh house is two-sloped. On both the sides of the sloping the walls support the roof and at the top end the roof is supported by the ridge pole (*tulipati*). The ridge pole in turn rests on the side wooden walls. In-between the ridge pole and the front wall as well as the back wall of the house, two horizontal bars are also passed overhead crossing the length of the house. At their ends they also rest on the side walls. These bars are called *depang pati*. Beyond the walls two horizontal bars one at the front and one at the back, serve as the outer support of the roof.

Though these horizontal beams rest on the extreme walls at their ends for greater support and safety of the roof, three smaller wooden posts (*makidinga*) are kept erect on the loft beam from the middle. After this broad outline of the roof is laid, small wooden bars (*kanda*) are placed from the ridge beam to the horizontal beams beyond the walls in slanting position. These rafters are laid close to each other and over it bamboo splints (*madipati*) are tied with strings of siali creeper (*paerdorr*).

The thatching material of the Malia house is not identical in nature though fired clay tiles are mostly in use. Some of the roofs are thatched with wild grass namely *biga* fetched from the forest in the months of January and February. Thatching of the roof is also made with a wild bush available in plenty from the forest namely *gazurka*. Some of the walls of the household have also tinsheets attached to wooden bars with suitable devices. Fired clay tiles (*khapars*) are purchased from the harijans of the neighbourhood at a cost of Rs. 175 for 1000 tiles. Nowadays Malias are skilled in preparing house tiles by means of a tile frame (*kaati*).

19

Household Objects

Badudi (Broom)

THE broom is made of twigs of a wild grass locally called *badudi*. The small rounded portion for the grip is called *mutti*. Mostly it is made by women particularly by the old ladies and young girls. These grasses grow in rainy months, and during winter women collect them in bundles by cutting the stems with the help of a small knife. The stems are interwoven with each other towards its root end one after another to make it like a long string. The woven portion is coiled round and tied by both of its ends to make the broom. It is used for sweeping the floor of the house. A broom costs Rs. 1.50. The durability of a broom is from three to four months.

Tambi (Measuring Bowl)

The bowl is a hollow piece of wood, the base of which is circular in shape. It is made of *piasal* wood. It is made by the Malias. A solid piece of wood is picked up and the wood is scooped out from inside by a chisel (*likudi*). The upper surface of it is smoothened with the knife. On the surface of it along the border of its orifice, geometrical art forms are carved out to give it a decorative look. It is used for measuring various food grains, viz. paddy, rice, mustard, etc. The cost of the bowl is Rs. 50. Nowadays the bowl has no practical use.

Dandi (Beaker)

The mouth of the beaker is circular in shape having a large ring of smooth surface. A string of *siali* creeper is tied to its neck for hanging or carrying purposes. A dried gourd with a small portion of its elongated part serves the purpose. The beaker is used for carrying water to the field in distant places. Apart from its use as a beaker, it is also used as a container for keeping numerous odd objects of the household. The durability of the beaker ranges from one to two years. The gourd (*dandi*) is plucked from a creeper grown by the Malia Kondhs in their fields (*bada*) adjoining their homestead lands.

***Jumbi* (Earthen Pot)**

The belly of the pot is wider in circumference having a small mouth and a narrow neck. The colour of the pot is black as it is a fired clay work. A string of *siali* creeper (*paerdorr*) is wrapped round its neck for carrying. The earthenware is made by the potter (*kumbhar*). The pot is used for collecting sap of date-palm trees (*sindhi malu*) and *sago* palm tree. The pot is tied to the trunk of the tree directing its mouth towards the cutting line from which the sap comes out. The collected sap is then brought home for drinking. The pot costs Rs. 5. It lasts for one or two years. Different art forms are depicted on the surface of its body.

***Laka* (Gourd Container)**

It is another type of container used for storing seeds and small things.

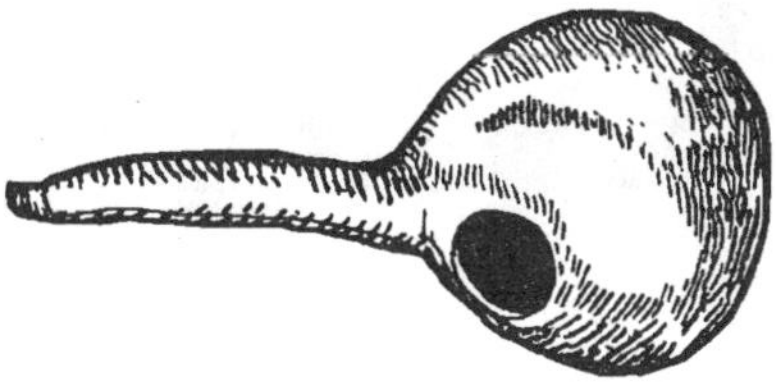

***Kele* (Knife)**

The knife has a wooden handle rounded in shape. The iron blade with a sharp and slightly curved edge, pointed towards the end, is made by the blacksmith while the handle is made at house by the owner. The iron blade is inserted into the wooden handle through the

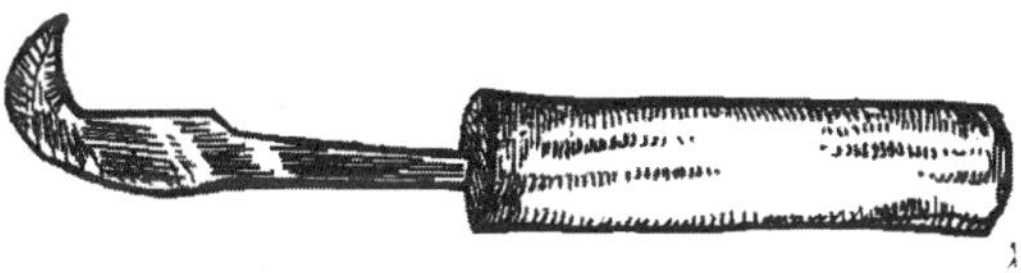

process of heating. It is used for cutting small branches of trees for fencing purposes and for feeding the goats, sheep, etc. Leaves of turmeric are also cut by this knife. The cost of the iron blade is Rs. 20. The durability of the implement is more than four years.

***Kude* (Knife)**

It is another variety of knife.

Sechu (Knife)

This knife has a long handle and a bent blade.

Gasa (Ladle)

The ladle consists of a thin bamboo split and fibres of cocoons. The ladles are made by men. The cocoon is cut at its upper end to carve out a circular mouth and is attached to the lower end of the bamboo split by lashing with the threads obtained from the same cocoon. The

ladle is used for taking out mohua liquor from a large receptacle and pouring it in the leaf cup for drinking. The object involves no cost in the preparation. The ladle lasts for three to four months.

Satuki (Ladle)

It is made of wood. One end of it is flat elongated to form a round handle.

Kolu (Pestle)

The pestle is made of wood. The foreshaft of the pestle is more in girth and round in shape while the bottom shaft is as rounded as to be gripped comfortably. An iron ring (*paredi*) is provided at the husking end and kept in tight grip. The mortar (husking hole) is generally

placed in the living room. The housewife while husking spreads both of her legs alongside the hole and releases the pressure of the pestle on the grains inside the hole using both of her hands by turn. The iron ring costs Rs. 7. It is made by the blacksmith and available at the local market. The pestle lasts for years together.

Martadi (Hammer)

This is an iron hammer with a long wooden handle.

Niju Gana (A Wooden Oil Press)

The oil press consists of two heavy planks of wood. One end of both the planks is inserted into the holes of a post. The wooden post holds the planks one above the other both horizontally placed slightly above the ground. The other ends of the planks are placed on a V-shaped pole. Both the posts (*plau*) are made of *mahua* wood (*irpi besku*). A handle (*tlau*) is fixed at the free end of the upper plank. On the side of the lower plank wood is scooped out to make a narrow channel for the oil to flow through. The press

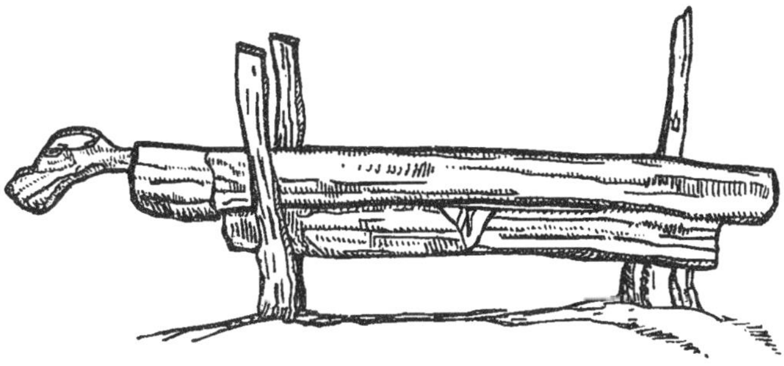

is made jointly by a group of Malias. The planks and posts are given the required shape by using axe and chisel.

The press is used for extracting oil from *mahua* seeds. The seeds are obtained and pounded by pestle to get its flour. Then the flour is fried and the fried flour is then kept in a tiny basket made of *siali* strings (*burki*) and placed in-between the planks. After the basket is placed, as many as eight to ten men press the upper plank. As the upper plank is heavier than the lower one, the resultant pressure facilitates extraction of oil flowing through the narrow channel. The oil is collected by keeping a receptacle on the ground beneath the lower plank. The construction of the structure involves no cost. Every adult male of the village contributes his labour in its making and it is owned communally. The press lasts for generations together.

20

Basketry

Guda (Bird's Cage)

THE cage is a simple basket work consisting of flexible bamboo wicks. A string of *siali* creeper is attached at the top for hanging. It is made by the basket maker, viz. *gudra*. Flexible bamboo wicks criss-crossing each other diagonally leave numerous holes in-between. It is used for keeping pet birds. The cost of the cage is Rs. 3. The cage lasts for a year or two. Mostly small birds are caught from the forest and kept inside this cage.

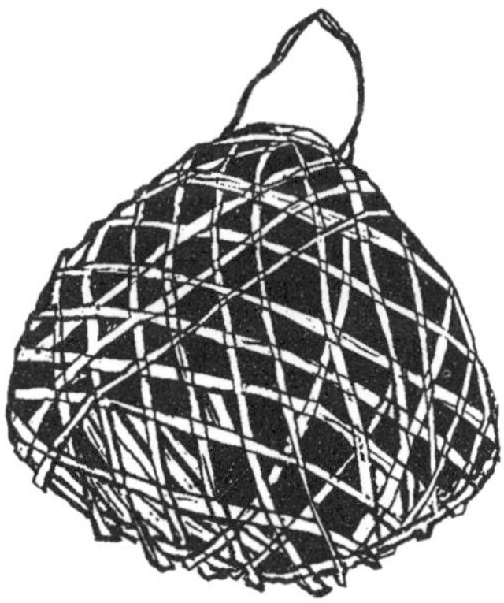

Diudi (Small Basket for keeping Tiny Fish)

This is a small piece of basketry of check pattern the base of which is semi-rectangular in shape. The hollow body is narrowed down. Its mouth is very small and rounded in shape. It is prepared by a Malia male skilled in bamboo work and involves a day's labour. As a first step flexible bamboo wicks are prepared by a knife. Wefts (horizontally woven) are passed under and over the warps (vertically placed) doubly.

Towards the middle of its body, rigid bamboo splints (four to five in number) pass obliquely under and over the warps doubly. The basket is used for keeping and carrying fish home after catching them from the streams and water-logged fields. The cost of the object is Rs. 12. The durability of the basket is five to six years.

As the scarcity of bamboo is felt in this area since long, the youngsters of present generations do not know basket making. A few Malia male of older age group, though engaged themselves in basket making, find it hard to earn a living from this small occupation due to scarcity of bamboo. This small basket is used only for a month or two particularly by the children when they enjoy trapping small fish from the water-logged paddy fields during the period lasting from sowing to transplanting. The basket is hung from the roof inside the house.

Dangeli (Basket for Keeping Things)

This basket is used for keeping vegetables and other items.

Binjuri (Basket for Keeping Things)

This is of a different shape and it is used like *dangeli*.

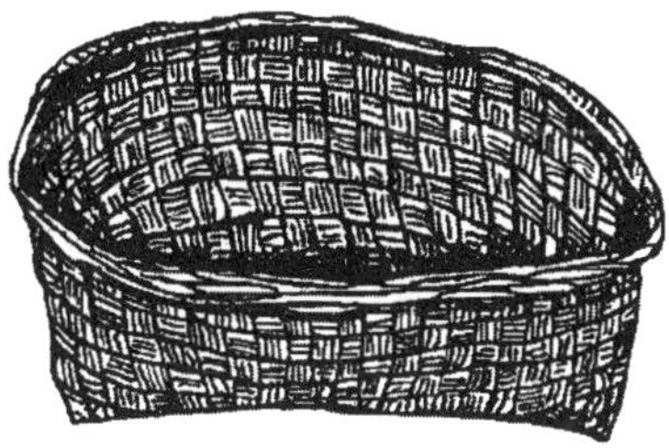

Buda Deba (Large Grain Bin)

The large grain bin is a piece of basketry square in shape. Stout bamboo warps are placed vertically at equal distance on all sides. Flexible bamboo wicks are woven horizontally under and over alternatively along the warps. It is made by the Malias who are skilled in basket work. It is used for keeping a large stock of paddy for future use and is closed at the top with straw plastered with cowdung mixed with mud. It involves no cost. It is placed in the main living room and lasts for years.

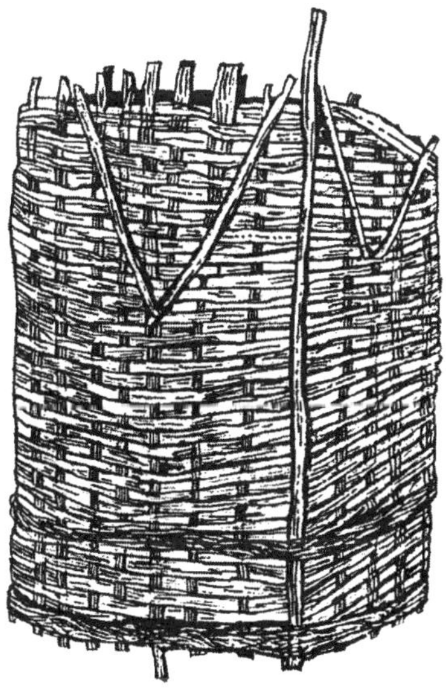

21

Food Quest

Wilu (Bow)

THE bow consists of an iron stave tapering towards both of its ends. The bow string is also a thin piece of iron plate made to form two loops at both of its ends. The loop is inserted at both ends into the stave notches. While using, the hunter holds the stave by the left grip and setting the arrownotch on the string and draws it towards him and releases the arrow towards the target. The cost of the bow ranges from Rs. 40 to Rs. 50 at the local market. The bow lasts for years. Sometimes during summer, the Malias go into the dense forest on a hunting expedition in groups carrying bows and arrows. The animals hunted are usually deer, *sambar*, *kutura*, etc. and brought home to offer them to *Jakiri*, the village deity.

Ambu (Arrow)

The arrow is a single piece of iron, the shaft of which is rounded in shape. The arrow head is triangular in shape and pointed. The shaft

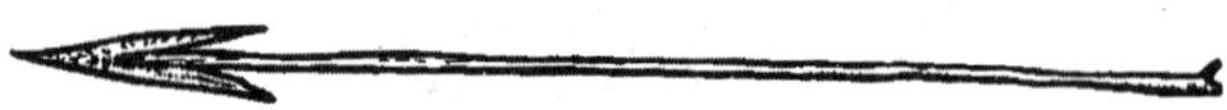

at its butt has a notch to set it on the bow string. The arrow is made by the blacksmith. The cost of the arrow is Rs. 5. The iron arrow lasts for years.

Giredi (Fish Trap)

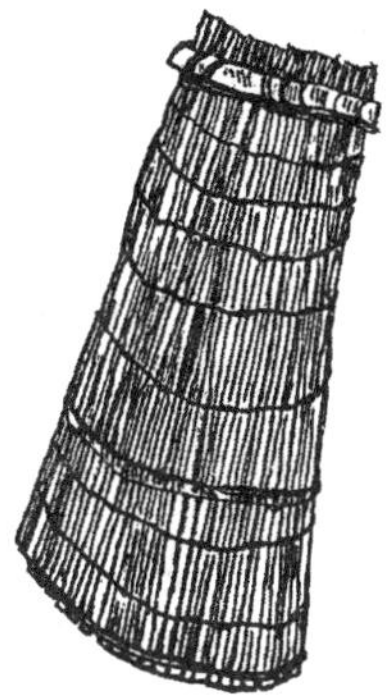

The fish trap has a wide open mouth narrowed down towards the closed end. It is made by the Malias. Strong bamboo sticks are held vertically in a line and tied with *siali* fibres passing each splint obliquely. At equal distance, the sticks are tied eight to ten rounds from the mouth to the closed end in a circular fashion. The mouth is kept wide open by means of a strong weft wrapped round its border and tied to the sticks by a string. The narrow end is kept closed. The trap takes a conical shape. In rainy season this trap is placed near a small stream. The mouth of the trap is directed against the flow of the stream. Small fish get trapped within it due to its closed end. The women use the trap for trapping fish from the agricultural fields. The trap involves no cost. It lasts for four to five years.

Sindu Kdalu (Glued Sticks for Catching Birds)

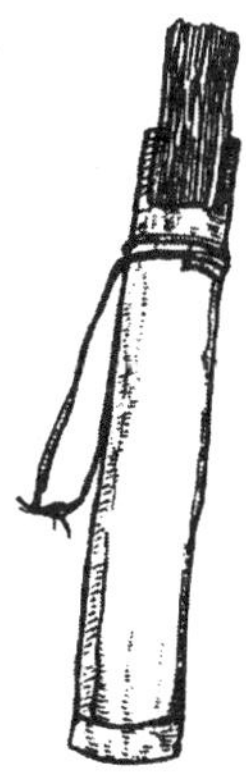

The container is a hollow piece of bamboo which is closed at one end by its natural joint and opened at the other end. The sticks are soaked in gum. The container is tied with a *siali* string at its mouth for hanging or carrying purposes. It is made by the youngsters. The gum is prepared by mixing the latex of peepal tree with the gum of banyan tree. As a next step, numerous bamboo splints are shaped into pointed sticks which are applied with gum. These sticks are set here and there in the branches of the fruit-bearing trees. While the birds perch on the sticks their legs get attached to the sticks and they find it difficult to fly and are caught easily.

It lasts for years though the gum is to be melted by heating it in the sun before its use. Except in rainy season, it is being used in almost every season. The trees which are full of small fruits and nuts are frequented by the birds.

Kujanga (Bird's Trap)

The trap consists of flexible bamboo splits bent from the middle and tied at the base by cotton threads. Again four pieces of the same thread are tied diagonally and run parallel to each other. A loop is prepared out of threads from the fibre of *sago* palm tree. The loop string is tied at the top of the bent bamboo split and the loop is kept hanging just at the middle gap of cotton threads. Fifty to sixty numbers

of such loop traps connecting each other by threads are fixed on the ground and two small bamboo sticks serve as support for the trap at both its ends to make the traps stand stretched.

The trap is made by the Malias. While using it, the bird-catcher sets the whole set of traps on the ground in a line and at both the ends it is tied with two slender bamboo sticks. As the cotton threads at the border obstruct the bird's way, it attempts to pass through the loop in the middle and as it moves away from the trap its body gets stuck inside the loop. The cost of the trap ranges between Rs. 20 to Rs. 25. The durability of the trap ranges from one to two years.

Tangari (Axe)

The axe consists of a wooden handle (*kloju*) rounded in shape made of *sal* wood and an iron blade with a sharp edge. The edge of the blade is slightly concave in shape while its body is convex in the middle. The head end of the shaft is inserted into a pointed brass cap. On the surface of the cap various arts are engraved for decoration. The iron

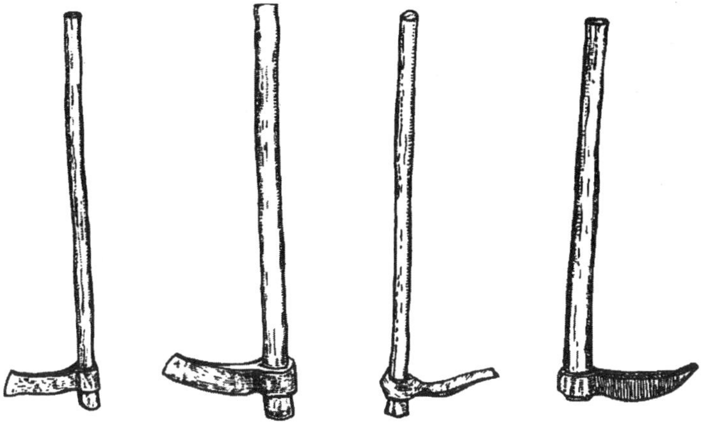

Kuradi *Tangari* *Gadaki* *Gadki*

blade and the cap are made by the blacksmith. The wooden handle is inserted into the blade socket and kept tight. The cost of the iron blade is Rs. 25. During one of their festivals, viz. *Kedu Parba* the males dance in groups by carrying the axe on their left shoulders. It is also used at the time of sacrificial offerings of goats, sheep, etc. before the deity. The axe lasts for generations.

Other varieties of axe are *gadaki*, *gadki* and *kuradi*, which are used for the same purpose as the *tangari* is used. All these types of axe are generally used for cutting wood particularly *kuradi* which is used mainly for cutting wood.

Pikasi **(Pick and Mattock)**

The pick and mattock consists of a wooden shaft (*kloju*) rounded in shape. The handle is fixed to the implement by means of a socket. The iron part is made by the local blacksmith, while the wooden handle is made by the user. The pick and mattock is used for digging earth and stony surface. The cost of the iron blade is more than Rs. 100 at the local market. The implement lasts for years together.

Rapa (Spade)

The spade consists of wooden shaft (*kloju*) shaped round and made of wood. The broad iron blade is locally called the *rapa*. The wooden shaft is made by any Malia male while the iron blade is purchased from the blacksmith. The socket of the broad iron blade is for the handle which is inserted into it and kept tight. The spade is used for earth work such as making bunds in agricultural fields, digging pits, spreading earth for levelling the village road, and digging foundation during house construction. The cost of the iron blade is Rs. 100. The wooden shaft of the spade is changed yearly while the blade lasts for years.

Nangeli (Plough)

The plough consists of two pieces of wood and an iron ploughshare. The beam (*kada*) is made of *sal* wood and shaped round. It is inserted into a hole made on the body of the plough and kept tight. The

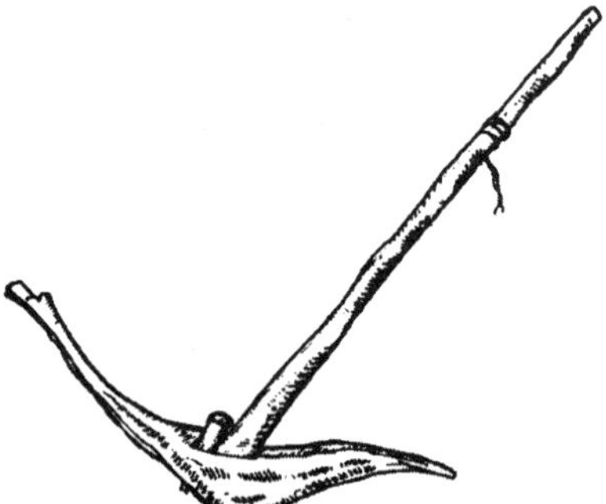

pointed iron share (*nangeli laha*) is fixed at the butt end of the wooden head. The plough is made by the Malias themselves. The beam is attached to a cross beam to which bullocks are harnessed for driving the plough. The cost of the iron share is Rs. 30 at the local market and the wood is fetched from the forest. The plough lasts for two to three years.

***Jueli* (Yoke)**

The yoke is made of *sal* wood. At both the ends two holes one in each end are made and two wooden pegs (*kilanga*) are inserted into the holes and fitted tight by iron-nails. A hole is bored at the upper part of each peg through which a rope passes. At the mid point of the yoke a U-shaped iron hook (*dagari*) is inserted. It is made by any

Malia male. While using it the yoke is placed on the shoulders of a pair of bullocks. The rope passes round the neck so as to keep the yoke in position. Beam of the plough is tied to the loop string attached to the U-shaped hook before ploughing. The iron nails are purchased from the market which costs Rs. 5. The durability of the implement ranges from five to six years.

***Patasingh* (Earth Leveller)**

The beam (*kada*) is rounded in shape and made of *sal* wood. The head end of the wooden beam is inserted into a hole made at the

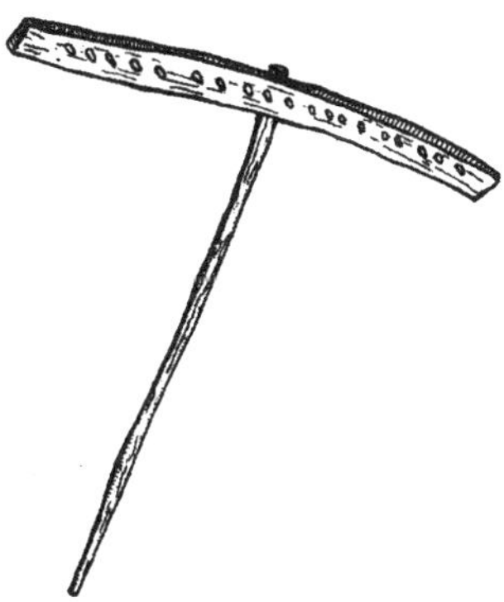

middle of another *sal* wood (*patasi*). A number of identical wooden pieces are fixed to the wood. It is made by the Malias. It is an agricultural implement tied to the cross beam (*juadi*) which in turn rests on the bullocks' shoulders. It is drawn by the bullocks to level the fields before the transplantation of paddy takes place. The leveller also picks up weeds and wild grass rendering the field clear of the weeds. The implement involves no cost, as wood is fetched free of cost from the forest. The implement lasts for some years.

Kurli (Earth Leveller)

This is another variety of leveller having a handle attached to a piece of wooden plank.

Kehele (Sickle)

The sickle has wooden handle and a bent blade serrated at the inner side.

Garka (Spear)

The spear has a long spearhead.

22

Personal Care, Dress and Adornments

Dress

HERE is nothing special to mention about the dress of men and women. Like the neighbouring Hindus the men wear *dhotis* and shirts and the women wear *saris* and blouses. Printed coloured sarees are generally used by the women. Red and blue coloured sarees are their favourite costume.

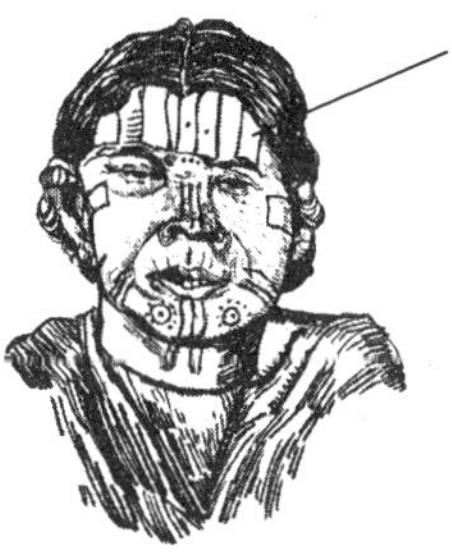

Tattooing

Hairstyle of a female

Tattooing is most common among the Kondh women. They get their face, hands and legs tattooed with dotted and line designs. There is a movement going on now prohibiting the practice of tattooing and many women of younger generation are found without any tattoo marks.

Pujupaka (Hairpin)

The women arrange their hair into a bun kept in position at the back of the head by means of hairpins.

The hairpin consists of a lengthy pin having a cap-like piece attached at its head end. The border of the cap is barbed. From the upper tip of the cap four to five chains are hung. The ornament is made of alloy of silver and brass. On the surface of the cap geometrical art forms are engraved. The hairpin is made by the *Ghasi* caste. During her marriage the bride uses the hairpin in her hair bun. At the various festivals females of younger generation adorn their hair with this ornament. The approximate cost of the hairpin is Rs. 20. The durability of the hairpin is for a lifetime.

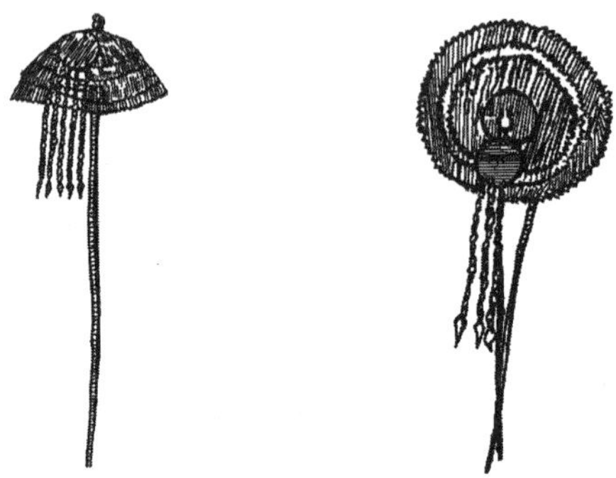

Kichedka **(Earring)**

The earring is made of a single silver wire shaped circular. It is made by the *Ghasi* caste. Since their childhood the girls have numerous perforations in their ear lobes. The rings are inserted into these holes. The cost of a ring is Rs. 2 per piece. The durability of the earring is more than eight years. As the ears get larger with advancement in age more perforations are made to use more rings.

Bala (Silver Bangles)

The bangles are made of silver. The joining ends are thicker than the other portion, and geometrical designs are carved on the body of the ornament. The ornament is made by the *Ghasi* caste. The bangle is inserted into the hand by opening wide the split ends and pressed afterwards to keep the bangle intact. Females of any age group can wear it in single or in pairs. The only ornament almost every Malia female uses in this silver bangle. The cost of the bangle is Rs. 10 a pair. The bangle lasts for a lifetime. After the death of the user, the dead body along with the ornaments is cremated. After some time the *Ghasis* collect these half burnt ornaments from the cremation ground and make new ones out of them for sale.

Biri Gagali (Anklet)

The anklet is made of brass. It is round and hollow inside containing brass pellets. The anklet is semi-circular in shape. On the upper surface of the ornament various designs are engraved. The ornament is made by the *Ghasi* caste. During marriage ceremony a pair of anklets adorns both the anklets of the bride which usually is a gift from her parents. The cost of a pair of anklets is Rs. 8. During a particular festival which is observed for a day, the men wear the anklets and dance. The pellets inside the anklets make sound while dancing.

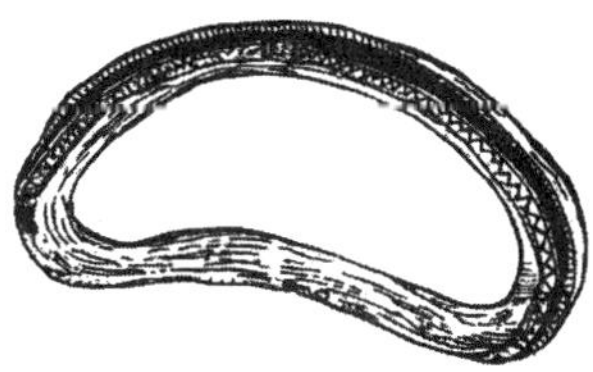

Sedi Kamanga (Horns made of Brass)

The ornament consists of a pair of brass-made horns hollowed inside. Towards its pointed end hollow pieces of brass are hung by hooks. The brass bells are fitted with small strikers suspended inside, so that they swing and strike the bells when the horns are shaken. It is made by the *Ghasi* caste. During marriage ceremony the ornament is given as a gift to the groom by his parents-in-law. The groom wears it over his head with the pointed parts facing upwards and tying it tightly by a piece of cloth wrapped round his head. As the relatives of the bride

carry the groom on their shoulder and dance, the bells produce different notes. The cost of a pair is Rs. 200. The ornament lasts for years together. Nowadays this ornament is rarely in use as all the specimens have almost been sold out to visitors for cash.

Gogla (Neck Band)

The neck band is made of brass. A woman wears more than one necklace which are made by the *Ghasi* caste.

23

Musical Instruments

Dala (Single Membrane Drum)

THE musical instrument consists of a hollow iron vessel. At its upper open end an iron rod rounded in shape is wrapped having four to five rings attached to it at equal intervals. The membrane stretched across the mouth of the iron drum is made of cow's hide. Two drumsticks (*dala kila*) made of the same skin is used for beating the drum. The iron vessel is made by the blacksmith while the hidework is done by the Malia male.

As the drum is heavy, it is hung by means of a piece of rope from a piece of wood carried by two men on their shoulders while the man at the back beats the drum with two drumsticks. It is used during festivals and marriage ceremonies. The cost of the iron base is Rs. 400 purchased from the blacksmith. Though the iron base lasts for years, the membrane is changed after ten to fifteen years.

Kanjari (Membrane Phone)

This is a circular shaped hollow piece of wood. On its surface two rectangular holes are made to weave a number of iron rings by an iron nail. The base is made of wood. The membrane prepared from the skin of a reptile is stretched across one of its side by a gum collected from a tree, called bengasi. It is made by the Malia male. While playing it, the user holds it by the left hand and beats the membrane with the right palm. The sounds emitted along with the rattling of the rings varies in pitch in accordance with the degree of tension the membrane gets. The iron rings costs Rs. 2 to Rs. 3. It lasts for a long time. During marriage ceremony and grand feasts it is played to the accompaniment of songs.

Sanga (Single Membrane Drum)

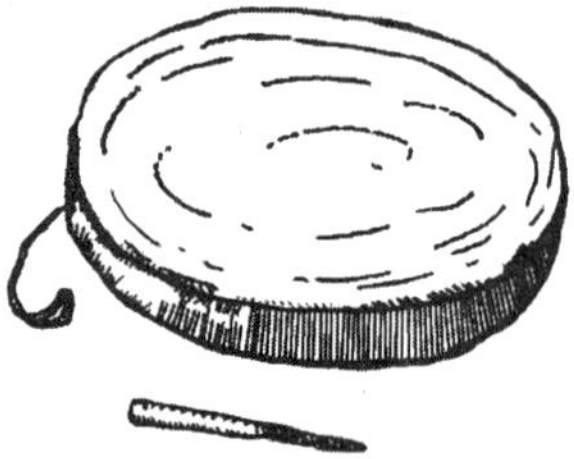

The drum consists of a rim of wood (*maduli*) of arjuna tree. On one side of the rim a membrane made of goat's skin is stretched and pasted by gum. Two drumsticks (*sanga kila*), one prepared out of *sisu* wood and another of a small piece of bamboo stick is used for beating the drum. Goat's skin is soaked in water for a day or two and the hairs are removed afterwards to get a smooth membrane out of it. The gum is prepared out of some roots. After stretching the membrane at one side of the rim it is pasted on the rim by the gum. The gum takes twenty-four hours to fix the membrane on to the rim.

The wooden rim is purchased from the market and the hide work is done by the user. The Malia male while playing it, hangs it on his left shoulder by a string. The lower surface of the rim rests on his left hand and both the hands are used for beating the drum. The drum is used in marriage ceremonies and *Meria* festival. The cost of the wooden rim is Rs. 60.00 at the local market. The drum lasts for a long time.

24

Religious Materials

Jakiri (Village Deity)

THE village deity consists of a wooden post. The post is carved on its surface with different art forms and split into two parts at its upper end. In front of it, a wooden pillar is posted. It is made by communal effort by all the Malias of a village. Men, and not women, shape the wood into a *Jakiri* post. During the numerous festivals particularly during the month of March and April it is worshipped by the village priest, and buffalo, goats and fowls are sacrificed as offerings to the deity for the well-being of the villagers. New posts are erected at two to three years interval.

Tangi (Axe)

The axe is exclusively used for sacrificing buffalo and other animals which are offered to the village deity on festive occasions.

Koru Koba (Wooden Post)

The sacrificial post consists of a wooden post carved out towards its upper half into three sectors. It is made by a Malia male. The post is fixed and used at the time of communal offerings of buffalo to the village deity (Jakiri). It is also kept inside the house. The Malia Kondhs believe that the disease and sufferings in the household are caused

by evil spirits. They sacrifice goat or fowl to appease them and overcome the difficulties. This post in front of the house serves as a sacrificial post for minor animals like goat, fowl, etc.

1. Kutia women

2. Young Dongaria girls

3. Dongaria lady with her nose rings

4. Dongaria girl in her traditional dress

5. Dongaria lady with her ornaments

6. Dongaria lady stitching her clothes

7. Dongaria man with his child

8. Dongaria boy with his bow

PART IV

Similarities and Variations

25

Similarities and Variations

As stated earlier the Kondhs are the largest tribal groups of Orissa, numbering over one million. There are roughly five sub-groups among them. They are: (1) The Kutia Kondh, (2) The Dongaria Kondh, (3) The Malia Kondh, (4) The Kuvi Kondh, (5) The Desia Kondh. The material culture of the first three sub-groups forms the subject matter of this publication. The differences and similarities of these three sub-groups are presented below.

The Kutia Kondh

The Kutia Kondhs live in remote hills in the extreme south-west of Phulbani district. This region covers Tumudi Bandha and parts of Kotagada block of the district. The study covers the Kutia Kondhs of Belghar area of Tumudi Bandha block. The Kutias are the 'Kui' speaking people. They understand Oriya language but it is more so among men than women.

The Kutia Kondhs are primarily shifting cultivators. They carry out this type of cultivation in the slopes of the hills which surround them. Though they have some contact with the Hindu neighbours yet they have kept their cultural traits intact.

The Dongaria Kondh

The Dongaria Kondhs inhabit the steep slopes of the Niyamgiri hill ranges of north-west Koraput district and the borders of Kalahandi district. The study covers those Dongaria Kondhs who inhabit the Niyamgiri hill ranges located in the Bissamacuttack region of Koraput district. This area comes under Chatikana block. The Dongaria Kondhs are 'Kuvi' speaking people. The Kuvi language is an extremely nasal form of the Kondh language. It consists of a few Telugu words.

Unlike other sub-groups of Kondh tribe the Dongaria Kondhs are famous horticulturists. They grow pineapple extensively in the hill slopes. The other fruit trees which are present locally are the mango trees and jackfruit trees. Banana, turmeric, and ginger are some of the other plants which they grow along with pineapples. The Dongaria country also has plantations of citrus plants like orange and lemon. The Niyamgiri hill ranges provide perennial hill streams which favour the Dongaria Kondhs in their plantation of fruit trees.

The Malia Kondh

The Malia Kondhs are larger in number than the Kutia Kondhs and the Dongaria Kondhs. They live in almost all parts of Phulbani district and west Gajapati district, but their main concentration is in Baliguda sub-division of Phulbani district. They are Kui speaking people like the Kutia Kondhs. The Kui dialect is much closer to Tamil than to Telugu. The Malia Kondhs understand Oriya language but they speak Oriya in a different fashion.

Unlike the Kutia Kondhs and the Dongaria Kondhs, the Malia Kondhs are primarily settled cultivators. They carry on wet cultivation in the plain lands around their settlements and mainly grow rice in the land.

Depending upon the economic condition, climate, terrain and occupation, the material world of these sub-groups presents a diverse picture from one sub-group to the other. These diversities are noticed in settlement pattern, house types, implements used in their occupational pursuits, dress and other traits of their material culture. The following paragraphs present these diversities as noticed in the different aspects of material culture.

The Kutia Kondh

Settlement Patterns and House Types

The Kutia villages are situated in the foot-hills or in the valleys surrounded by densely forested high hills. A village has two rows of houses flanked by a narrow village street. The village conforms to the east-west setting of the rows of houses in a linear pattern. The houses of one row face towards north and those of the other row towards south. Conspicuous in the village are the youth dormitories for young men and women which are built at the end of the rows of houses. Cattle sheds are built separately at the back of the houses.

The Kutia Kondhs build their houses on a rectangular ground plan. A Kutia house consists of a single room partitioned inside into two parts, one part set apart as kitchen and the other part used as a living room. In some cases it is partitioned into three parts. The walls are made of *sal* saplings plastered with mud on both sides. The roof is covered with locally made tiles. The floor of the house is about two feet below the level of the village road and this low lying floor of the house is called *kuti* which has given the name to the tribe as Kutia Kondh. Each house has a verandah in front which is used as sitting place. Recently the verandah has been divided into two parts. One part is used as a guest room and the other side used as a sitting place.

The house is provided with two doors one in front and the other at the back. The mortar in which rice is pounded is fixed into the floor at the middle of the living room. The Kutia Kondhs pound rice and other grains in the mortar by means of a pestle.

There is an extra room built for the womenfolk to retire during the menstrual cycle. In some villages there may be four to five such rooms available for common use. Many women enjoy the facility of such common accommodation even though they have provision in their own houses. These rooms when free are used by the household as goat shed or pig sty.

At the middle of the village is installed the *Dharani Penu* and *Karumunda*. It is the tradition that the *Dharani Penu* and *Karumunda* should be placed almost at the middle of the village and therefore any extension of the village on either end is not allowed because it will distort the seat of the deity.

The space at the back of the house is used for kitchen garden, and the sheds of domestic animals are also constructed there. Most of the Kutia villages have jackfruit trees which are considered auspicious. Salap trees (*Caryota urens*) are also found in the area of settlement.

In every village there must be one or two families of Domb or Pano community. The members of this community tend the cattle of the Kutia Kondhs. Their houses are located at a little distance from the main village. At the extreme end of the village is the place for depositing garbages. Sometimes compost pits are found at such places.

Each Kutia Kondh village was formerly composed of a single clan. But it has become now multi-clan in composition. Traditionally the people with Jani surname used to live in one row and the people bearing the Majhi surname lived on the other row. But at present people of both surnames are living mixed in different rows.

Household Objects

JHATRA (*SIPERI* AND *PRANG JHATRA*) BROOM

The Kutia Kondhs use brooms made of two different kinds of materials. In one case a kind of broom grass locally called '*satrangi*' is used and this type of broom is called *siperi jhatra*. The strands of the grass are dried and tied into small bunches to make the brooms. In the other case the twigs of a bushy plant which are dried and thereafter are tied into small bunches to make the broom which is called *prang jhatra*.

KADELI (STRING COT)

Every Kutia Kondh house must have one or two such cots which are called *kadeli*. The strings used for this cot are nothing but the fibres collected from *siali* creeper plant called *Bauhinia vahlii*. The frame of the cot including the legs are made of wood which is locally available.

GUNJER BALI (QUERN)

Besides the above two essential materials every household must have a quern locally called *gunjer bali*. The quern consists of two circular stones. One stone is fixed to the ground with a peg fixed into it in the centre and the other which is heavier is laid on the stone fixed into the ground. The upper and heavier stone is kept in position by fixing it to the central peg of the ground piece. An L-shaped wooden peg is inserted into the hole made on the side of the upper heavier stone. This peg serves as the handle. The Kutia housewife, in a sitting posture, inserts grains through the hole at the centre and rotates the upper stone by means of the handle in a clockwise direction on the lower one. The grains in-between come out in powder form through the small space between the stones.

KALLU (MORTAR & PESTLE)

For the purpose of husking certain grains the pestle and mortar are used. The mortar is imbedded on the floor of the front verandah or in the main living room. The housewife inserts grains like paddy or wheat which are to be husked. She does this work in a sitting posture. She pounds the grains by means of the pestle. She uses both her hands for this purpose. She puts the grains in with her right hand and pounds the grains with the left hand. The pestle which is made of wood has different geometrical art-forms which are carved out on the surface.

Besides these material objects there are many other things found in the house of a Kutia Kondh. These are *terka danga* (a wooden device for pounding bamboo shoots), *mara set* (ladle), *serbebali* (curry-stone), *nakudi danga* (wooden container), *mani duna* (bamboo container), *simba dapra* (ladle for serving gruel), *madang dana* (leaf cup), *dua duna* (tobacco container), *maso parang titudi* (gourd container), *kare* (knifes).

BASKETRY

The Kutia Kondhs make baskets of various types and sizes to store their foodstuff, to collect forest produce and for various other purposes. They use bamboo splits of different thicknesses and use various techniques of weaving them into baskets. Braided and interwoven objects are found in large numbers. The wicker work of twilling pattern is used to make baskets which are used for drying minor millets and seeds of different crops. Certain baskets such as grain bin show wicker work on the body and coiled narrow belt in different places providing strength to the basket.

Large grain bins are made using check pattern in which each weft passes over and then under each warp in a circular bend. The bags are made of bamboo splits using wicker work pattern with coiled ropes supporting the bag.

Siali creeper is also used for making baskets particularly bags of different sizes. The ropes of *siali* creepers are woven by means of sewing needles made out of bamboo. Such bags are of twilling pattern. Mats are also made using bamboo splits. Flexible wefts pass over and under alternately to give a twilling pattern. Shutters made of bamboo splits of wicker work are common types of basketry found among the Kutia Kondhs. Fencing is done using bamboo splits using the pattern of wicker work.

Food quest

The main occupation of the Kutia Kondhs is shifting cultivation. Various crops are grown in a hill slope for two or three years and then the plot is abandoned for a few years to recuperate. Wherever plain lands are available these lands are also used for growing crops. The implements used in shifting cultivation are a hand hoe, dibble, spade, and sickle. But when plain lands are cultivated the cattle-drawn plough is used. The plough is now used in hill slopes also. In plain lands levellers are used to level the surface of the land which is ploughed.

A plough consists of two pieces of wood, one piece forming the handle, body and plough share and the other forming the beam which is slightly curved against the body of the plough. The plough share is made of iron whereas other parts are made of wood. The free end of the beam is tied to the yoke to which bullocks are harnessed for driving the plough.

PICK AND MATTOCK

The pick and mattock is made of iron and it consists of a handle which is made of wood. The handle is fixed to the socket of the pick and mattock and by means of this tool, dry and hard earth is dug. The pickside is pointed and the mattock side is broad.

Besides these main tools sickle is used for harvesting crop. It is made of iron which is fitted to a wooden handle.

FISHING IMPLEMENTS

The main implement used for fishing is a trap. It is a kind of trap which falls in the category of basketry having its middle portion bulging and the neck portion narrowed down so that the fish falling into the trap find it difficult to get out of it. The trap is set in a place where water flows from the higher level to the lower level.

HUNTING IMPLEMENTS

Bow and arrow are the main implements used for killing animals. It is a simple device consisting of a curved bamboo staff and the string made of fibre. The arrow consists of a slender reed and the head, a triangular piece of pointed iron blade with the lower part flattened so that it can pierce into the body of the targeted animal. The feathers of peacock are tied at the butt-end with cotton threads or cocoon strands to give it a smooth flight when shot. The notch for the lower string is cut at the butt end of the reed.

BIRD CATCHING DEVICES

The gum-coated sticks are used for catching birds. The sticks are made of slender bamboo splits and gum is collected from plants. The gum-coated sticks are tied to the branches of trees like banian during fruiting time and spread on the ground near paddy fields when the crops are ready for harvesting. When the birds sit on the branches to eat the fruits or when they fly over the paddy fields to eat the crops they get stuck to these sticks, find it difficult to fly away, and fall an easy prey to the bird-catchers.

Various types of snares are set on the ground to catch the birds. The snare by means of which wild fowls are caught is called *kajukuting*. It consists of some loops made of fibres of *sisal* plant. These loops are separately tied to a strong string in a line. One end of the string is tied to a stump and the other end to another stump thus keeping the snare tight and straight and in a line. A cock is tied to the loop as a bait which attracts the birds which come flying to fight with the bait. Generally the jungle fowls are attracted by the sound when the cock crows. While fighting, the legs of the jungle fowls get caught in the loop. In its attempt to become free from the snare the loops get tightened rendering it impossible for the fowl to escape.

Personal Care, Dress and Adornments

DRESS

A Kutia Kondh male wears a loincloth. The cloth covers only the lower private part of the body. He does not use any cloth to cover the upper part.

The clothes used by the women consist of three pieces covering the upper part of the body which is nothing but a towel hanging in front up to the thigh. The second piece is a loin cloth which covers the private part of the body. It is tied to the string of the waist. The third piece is nothing but a skirt used to cover the loin. The hair in the case of a woman is arranged into a knot at the back of the head.

The traditional dress pattern has undergone changes. Now the male members use modern dress like pants, trousers and shirts. Similarly the women have replaced the upper apron with blouses and wear printed sarees. They use ornaments made of gold, silver, brass, aluminium and plastics. These ornaments consist of ear and nose rings, necklaces and anklets.

The women have their arms tattooed with geometrical and floral designs. The tattoo marks on the body are for the sake of improving the beauty of a woman. They also use bangles and waist belts, and hair-pins in the bun.

Musical instruments

The common musical instruments which are used by the Kutia Kondhs are pellet bells attached to hollow pieces of bamboo. Rattle, flute and single membrane drums are common. A kind of rattle made out of a dried fruit with seeds inside make sonorous sound. Clappers are also used as musical instruments.

Religious Objects

The speciality of the Kutia Kondh is the mother goddess which is installed in the middle of the village street. The deity is represented by three pieces of stone kept within a bamboo enclosure. During *Kedu* festival, a buffalo is sacrificed while worshipping the mother goddess.

There is also another village deity called *Dehu Penu* which is installed in a shrine at the entrance of the village.

There is a wooden deity consisting of a single piece of *sal* wood. A bell is hung in the notch at the upper end of this wooden object. This deity is placed adjoining the right side wall of the living room. There is a sacrificial post called *Meria pole* which is fixed on the ground in the village street of every Kutia village. The buffalo which is sacrificed is tied to this pole and the Kutias, while celebrating the occasion, hack the animal with an axe as a part of the *Meria* festival.

The Dongaria Kondh

Settlement Patterns and House Types

The Dongaria Kondh village is situated wherever there is a shelf in the steep hills or in a gentle slope at the foothills. Every village has a long and wide street running in east-west direction. The houses are built close to one another on either side of the village street and face each other. In some villages there may be two or more such double rows of houses existing at a little distance from the main street.

Everywhere the Dongaria Kondh village is set in the east-west direction. There is a reason for such setting. The Kondhs believe that the presence of their Creator-Sustainer Deity symbolized by the sun is necessary at all times for their well being and harmony in villages. The presence of sunlight can be maximized by setting the village street in the east-west direction. Moreover, this east-west setting of the rows which enforces north-south setting of each household in each row ensures sharing of sunlight equally by all the households.

There is another benefit of this east-west setting of the rows of houses. Such a setting has a warm side in winter and it is very pleasant to do household chores. Also being set on a slope, rain water drains off rapidly without flooding the houses and the village streets, thus keeping them clean all the time. In other seasons the heat of the sun dries up the soil and removes dampness, a condition which deters the spread of diseases.

In the village itself, though detached from the Kondh houses, there is a cluster of Domb houses, set in rows in the same east-west direction. The Domb is a Scheduled Caste and indispensable in the life of the Kondhs. The Kondh *sahada* (section or ward) and the Domb *sahada* are flanked by an open space having heaps of stones serving as cowsheds for some houses. In some villages these *sahadas* are in two terraces one lower than the other separated by the steep fall of the terrace.

On one end, away from the village, is the cremation ground; one for the Kondhs and another for the Dombs. Situated on either side of the village road is the *Jatra Kudi* (shrine of a deity represented by wooden poles) and a little ahead of it, is the abode of *Thakurani* (Goddess of the village) enshrined in a small thatched hut.

Either ahead of the abode of *Thakurani* or at the back of any row of houses the dancing ground is located in some convenient place. The village community hall-cum-the temple of *Jahir*, Earth Goddess or *Sadar Kudi* as it is called, is present in some place in the street. The girls' dormitory is always built at the back of any of the two rows of houses preferably close to the stream or river flowing nearby. From the village start roads leading to different neighbouring villages. There are hills on all sides of the village with plantations of fruit-bearing plants and trees in the hill slopes. Patches of shifting cultivation are also met with in the hill slopes preferably in higher altitudes.

Dongaria Kondh House

When a Dongaria Kondh wants to build a house in his own village he does not have to obtain permission from the villagers if he belongs to their *Mutha*. But if he wants to build a house in another village which is outside his own *Mutha* he has to obtain permission from the village elders before he starts building the house. Previously the households of a village belonged to a single *Mutha* but this homogeneity has broken down and in its place the village has become heterogeneous, in the sense that people of different *Muthas* are found living in the same village.

Before taking up the construction of the house the first work which he does is the clearing of the place where the house is to be built. If there are trees, bushes and shrubs on the ground he cuts them, clears them and levels the ground. Then comes the divination which is performed to test the suitability of the site for habitation.

The main ingredients of the divination are a branch of *saragi* tree and some rice. On any Sunday, the Kondh takes bath early in the morning and proceeds to the nearby forest in search of a *saragi* tree. In some cases they consult a *Bejuni* (a foreteller) and start at an auspicious moment for this purpose. He has to select a *saragi* tree which must fulfil the following conditions:

1. The tree should not be bare of leaves;
2. The tree must be unaffected by insects;
3. The tree should not be having any nest of any bird;
4. It must be a healthy tree with branches and green leaves.

Once he has located a tree of the above-mentioned specifications, he gives his first stroke by his axe on a stout branch and waits to listen if any hissing sound is made by the tree. If he hears no sound, then he proceeds in his work of cutting a branch of the tree. Then he shapes the branch to make a post of 4 ft to 5 ft in length. With the post resting on his shoulder he walks back to his house without looking back.

After two days, that is, on the Wednesday in the morning after bath, he digs a pit in the middle of the plot which is cleared for the construction of the house and sets the post in the pit with about a foot of the post being buried in the pit.

The same day in the evening he keeps five or seven grains of white rice near the post and covers them with a leaf of *siali* creeper plant (*Bauhinia*). Next morning, that is on Thursday, he observes these grains. If he finds that the grains are not at all disturbed and they are in the same position as they were the previous day, he takes it as a good omen which goes in favour of building his house on the site.

This is not enough to determine the suitability of the plot for building the house. Now the testing will centre around the post which was fixed in the pit in the middle of the plot. After about a week the post will be examined and if it is found that no ants or insects have damaged the post it is a good sign and he will take a final decision to build the house.

After the site is selected by the process of testing omens he sets out to get the required number of posts which are used in the construction of the house. In a Dongaria Kondh house as many as 60 wooden posts or wooden pillars (*munda*) are required and it takes nearly a week or so for a Kondh to collect these posts from the forest. In fact, these posts are cut and kept in the jungle long before the house is constructed. It is only when the construction starts that these posts are hauled from the forest to the construction site.

Before the posts are set in appropriate places, the Kondh does some carvings or designs on the wooden posts. It may be noted that the Dongaria Kondhs are experts in wood carving. The carvings made on the post testify the manual skill of the Kondhs.

The next item of work is the fixing of these wooden posts in their respective places. First of all two posts, one in the eastern side and the other on the western side of the house, are fixed in the middle of the plot. These posts are called *munumunda* which are the longest among all other posts. Generally, these *munumunda*s are each 13'6" in length. Nearly 3 ft of the post remains buried in the pit and the remaining 10'6" above the ground. A beam of 13'6" is fixed on these two posts. The room which will be constructed in the centre of the plot is called *eja* and it is in the side walls of *eja* that the *munumunda*s are fixed.

On the northern side and the southern side of the *munumunda,* 20 posts (*patimunda* — 10 on each side) are fixed on the ground. It means five posts in the east and five posts in the west on the northern side and similarily five posts in the east and five posts in the west on the southern side are fixed along the lines of *munumunda*. These 10 posts on each side gets shorter and shorter in height and a beam is fixed on each pair of these posts.

Then five posts are fixed along the line which will be the back wall of the front room which is called *duki*. The posts are named as *dukimunda*. One beam runs over these five *dukimundas*. According to the Dongaria Kondh, the height of the *dukimunda* will be equal to the height of a man. Likewise five posts are fixed in the back wall on the rear room which is called *dapa* and therefore the posts which are fixed in this room are called *dapamunda*. A beam runs over these *dapamundas* from side to side of the house.

For the front verandah which is called *asana pinda,* six *mundas* — three in front and three at the back — are fixed on the ground and a beam is set on the three posts in front and another beam is set on the three posts at the back side. Likewise six posts are fixed in the back verandah which is also called *asana pinda*. Two beams, one on three posts in front and the other on the three posts at the back are fixed.

Inside the house, four posts — two in the northern side and two in the southern side — are fixed and a beam is fixed on each pair of these posts. The purpose of putting the beam on these posts is to enable the rats to move along these beams. These posts are called *arakimunda*. Similarly three *arakimundas* are fixed in the *duki* room and three in *dapa* room each supporting a beam for the movement of the rats.

There is an inner chamber called *kandadaya* in the south-eastern corner of the living room or central room or *eja*. This *kandadaya* is situated in front of the hearth which is located in the south-western corner of the room. This inner house has three posts on the eastern side and three on the western side. The posts in the east support one beam and the posts on the west support another beam. This chamber has walls on three sides and is open on the hearth side.

The central room has an overhead loft. To support this loft, four posts — two on the southern side and two on the northern side with supporting beams — are fixed on the ground. There is an opening in the loft just above the hearth, and a post with steps carved on it is fixed on the ground in-between the hearth and the inner chamber. The post is used as a ladder to climb up to the loft.

Another small loft is provided immediately above the hearth. This loft is used for keeping foodstuff such as *ragi*, mutton, flesh of buffalo, etc. which requires drying before cooking. The overhead loft which is provided above the living room is used as a store where agricultural and forest produce, clothes, ornaments and other household possessions are kept in safety. Long bamboos are placed side by side closely on the beams which are supported by posts making the floor of the loft. It is plastered both sides with mud to give a smooth surface. The loft is set at such a low height that a man cannot stand erect in the room.

The wall is made of wooden poles plastered with mud. These poles are fixed on the ground in-between the posts which support the beams from one side of the house to the other side in east-west direction. The front wall of the front room facing the front verandah and the outer wall of the back room facing the back verandah are constructed by using self-made sun-dried bricks. These brick walls are also plastered with mud.

The roof of the house is of gabled type in the sense that it slopes down on both sides from the ridge pole. Among the Dongaria Kondhs the east-west setting of the rows of houses on either side of the village street (*raha*) ensures that every house is sloped in the north-south direction. The rafters are of bamboos which are fixed to the beams starting from the ridge pole to the eaves of the house. A hole is made at the end of the rafter which rests on the ridge pole and a peg is inserted through it. This peg anchors the ridge pole and gives security to the rafter. Similarly, pegs are also provided in the lower parts of the rafter for anchorage with the beam below for greater security. Bamboo splits are laid over and under the rafters and tied at several places by means of *siali* fibres. This roof trellis slopes steeply on both sides of the house. It is thatched with a kind of locally grown grass called *piri*.

After all these works are done, a pestle (*hena*) in the central living room (*eja*) and another in the rear room (*dapa*), are embedded in the ground. It is in these pestles that the grains are pounded by means of a mortar. Near the pestle to a side in some convenient place a rotary quern (*jatabali*) is placed. The raised earthen platform in the north-western of the living room is used for keeping the earthen lamp.

In front of the inner chamber towards the north-eastern corner, the oven (*hulu*) is placed. It is a twin-oven fed by firewood through a single mouth. The smoke which emits rises straight into the loft overhead through the passage which is located just above the oven. Immediately above the hearth is a small loft over which food grains such as *ragi*, maize and non-vegetarian foodstuff such as mutton, buffalo flesh and fish which require dehydration are kept so that the heat of the oven dries them up. Close to the eastern wall near the hearth, an earthen platform (*ayupinda*) is made on which cooked food, cooking vessels and water pots are kept.

The household shrine (*kondanake*) is installed in the inner chamber which is called *kondodoe*. Outside this chamber in the side wall facing the living room some shelves are provided. Things like winnowing fan (*hechi*) used for magico-religious purposes and occult rice containers (*mole tinguli*) are kept in these shelves. A seat (*hondenikudo*) is provided nearby where occulticism is practised whenever required.

The front room called *duki* is used for sitting and entertaining guests. No outsider is allowed to enter the house beyond this room. A loft is provided either in the western side or in the eastern side for the pigeons to sit. The space under the loft is used as the fowl pen. The corresponding room at the back called *dapa* is the secluded ante-room where the women of the house spend their time. During the menstruation period they are secluded in this room. One or two pestles are present in this room for the women to pound the food grains. Various household possessions are kept in the western side of the room and the pig sty is present on the eastern side. The entrance into this enclosure is at its backside and the pigs get into this enclosure through the back verandah. But an opening is provided in the western side wall through which feed is given by the women to the pigs.

There are two verandahs (*asana pindas*) — one in front and the other at the back. The front verandah is an important part of the house. It serves many social and economic purposes. In the back verandah the women clear the grains before pounding, prepare vegetables, make leaf-plates and gather to chat with one another with babies in the lap, comb their hair and adorn themselves. Similarly men spend time in the front verandah on various activities such as mending equipment, chit-chatting with the neighbours, smoking and lounging particularly in the case of old men. Scaring away the chickens so that they do not eat up the grains dried on the ground, and watching the passersby and interacting with them if and when needed, are some of their other passtime activities.

The Dongaria house is built with a low roof-ridge and with eaves drooping down low (less than four feet from the ground level) over a high verandah. The same architecture is noticed both in front and at the back of the house. This makes entry possible only in a crouching position but the house is spacious within. These architectural peculiarities of lower roof-ridge, very low eaves and high verandah of the Dongaria house are of great utility in the sense that the low eaves prevent damage caused to the mud wall by the splashing of rain water. Moreover more heat is retained for hearth thereby making the indoor life pleasant and comfortable in a cooler climate all the year round and especially in severe cold winters.

A house of this type will have four doors — the front door leading to the *duki* room, second door to the *eja* room, the third to the *dapa* room and the rear door leading to the back verandah. These doors are fixed in a single line almost in the middle of the rooms. It is the work of the men to make such heavy doors which pivot on a wooden peg set into a small hole made in the floor. There is a system of locking the front door and the back door. No window is provided in any room. Sometimes the *dapa* may have a window set in the front wall opening in the front verandah. But it is rarely met with.

Cattle shed is built separately at the back of the house. A low wooden platform at a height of about four feet above the ground is made and screened off on all the sides by means of plaited bamboo wicker work with the entrance facing the back side of the house. A slightly sloping passage is provided over which the cattle tread on into the shed.

After the construction of the house is over and before it is occupied a ritual is performed for the health and happiness of all the members of the household. It is performed on any Wednesday as fixed by the sorcerer (*Bejuni*) and village head. The things which are required in the ritual are a new winnowing fan, a white cock, two brown cocks, a white pigeon and a gourd ladle in which *ragi* is kept. Two small containers with cover are also needed. White rice is kept in these containers.

On the day of the worship in the morning, *Bejuni* goes out to the outskirts of the village to propitiate the deity residing in the patch leading to the village. The owner of the house and other members and a few relatives proceed to the place of worship and welcome him back to the house. Welcoming him back means to welcome the Goddess Lakshmi to the house. While returning, the *Bejuni* carries with him a new piece of cloth in which some white rice is tied and holds under his armpit a fowl. As soon as the *Bejuni* reaches the doorstep of the house, turmeric water is sprinkled over him. Thereafter, the *Bejuni* gets into the house and starts worshipping the deities residing in the house. The ancestors are also worshipped on this occasion. This ritual is attended by the relatives of the houseowner and all the villagers and the ceremony is brought to a close with a community feast in which all present take part.

Household Objects

JATA BALI (GRINDING STONE)

The Dongaria Kondhs use the quern to grind the grains as the Kutias do. But in their case the quern is semi-circular in shape and both the pieces of stone are the same in weight. The bigger piece is half buried in the ground and the other piece is rotated on the ground piece. The upper piece is kept in position over the ground piece by means of a hole in the former through a stump fixed in the centre of the latter. The housewife, in her sitting posture, rotates the upper piece over the ground piece by means of the wooden handle which is fixed into the upper piece of stone.

KALU (MORTAR AND PESTLE)

The bottom end of the pestle is fitted with an iron ring. The mortar is fitted into the hole made in the floor of the living room. The upper part of the wooden pestle is solid and thick intended for putting heavy pressure on the grains while husking. This thicker part of the pestle is carved with hexagonal design. Most of the Dongaria women prefer to do the husking work in the mortar fixed in the hut of the spinster's dormitory.

Besides these objects, there are several other objects found in the house of a Dongaria Kondh. Some of these materials are *hatudi* (bamboo and leaf hat), *ada* and *manda* (measuring brass and wooden bowl), *dumuni* (serving ladles), *dumuni* (gourd), *sunga* (Tobacco pipe), *madi duna* (bamboo container), *mada kalu* (beaker), *takurani* (lamp post), *pitda dipi* (lamp), *badti* (lamp stand), *dipi* (hanging lamp stand), *tatkadi* (cowbell), *suri* (knife), *khanda* (sword), *madla* (wooden hammer).

BASKETRY

The Dongaria Kondhs use various types of baskets for different purposes. The basket which is used for carrying minor forest produce and other things is called *unga katra*. It is made of flexible bamboo wicker work. The wefts pass under and over the warps singly and alternatively. The rim of the basket is coiled bamboo work as four members of wefts pass in front and behind each of the warps crossing them obliquely. It is kept hanging from the loft by means of strings.

There are baskets which are used for keeping vegetables and certain baskets are used for carrying pellets. Most of the baskets are kept hanging from the loft by means of strings.

There is a basket of the shape of a cap. It is used for covering meat or fish while drying them in the sun, so that the crows do not take them away.

Since the Dongaria Kondhs do not grow paddy, they do not have baskets which are used for storing grains. Most of their baskets are used either for carrying forest produce or for storing them at home.

Since bamboo is not available in their locality they purchase the baskets from the market.

FOOD QUEST

The main occupation of the Dongaria Kondhs is horticulture. They grow, in the hill slopes, turmeric and ginger. The fruit-bearing trees and plants which they grow are mango, jackfruit, banana, lemon, orange and pineapple. Extensive hill slopes in the Bissamacuttack hills which are the habitat of the Dongaria Kondhs have such plantations. For this purpose they rarely use plough because ploughs do not work in the steep hill slopes. The implements which are very common among the Dongaria Kondhs in their quest for food are handhoes. Other implements used in their practice of horticulture are axe and adze. There are various types of axes which are mainly used for cutting trees and clearing bushes. The adze is also used for cutting trees and cutting wood into small pieces, which are used as fuel. They also have spades with which they dig earth and spread them after breaking them into small pieces.

HUNTING IMPLEMENTS

The Dongaria Kondhs use pellet bow and other types of simple bow and arrows. The pellet bow is used for releasing clay pellets towards the target. Ordinary bows are used to shoot arrows at the animals for killing. The arrow has a shaft to which the head is fixed at one end. The head is a thin triangular piece of iron blade having sharp edges on two sides. The other end of the shaft has a notch which is either single shouldered or double shouldered. At this end feathers of fowls are tied by means of skin cords or by cotton threads.

The Dongaria Kondhs use various types of wooden clubs. It is carried by them when going out to the field. The club is generally used as an offensive as well as a defensive weapon. They have also spears with which they kill animals particularly poisonous snakes.

Though the Dongaria Kondhs do not grow crops by cultivation, those who live close to lands in the plains use cattle drawn ploughs.

They also use sickle to harvest the crops, but these implements are very rare among the Dongarias.

TRAPS AND CAGES

The Dongarias use a kind of trap by means of which they trap the rabbits. The trap consists of several loops which are kept hanging in a line in a string which is fixed to the ground by stretching it tightly and tying both the ends to nearby stumps of trees. The trap is just like the loops used by the Kutias for catching birds. The Dongarias have cages in which they keep birds which are caught from forest.

Personal Care, Dress and Adornments

DRESS

The dress of both men and women among the Dongaria Kondh is very peculiar, so that one can distinguish them among other tribal groups.

A Dongaria male uses a long cloth covering the private part of his body. It is wound round his waist and the front portion is kept hanging in front. Similarly the part which is kept hanging at the back is shorter in length than the part which is kept hanging in front. The men cover the upper part of their body with scarfs embroidered by the Dongaria women. The adornment of a Dongaria male consists of a comb which is kept in position in the hair on the head.

Every Dongaria man will have a knife which has a small wooden handle attached with a tin blade having a sharp edge. The Dongaria man also uses hairpins to keep the hair in position. The Dongaria women use a saree which covers both the lower and the upper part of the body. She also covers the upper part of the body with a scarf with embroidery work on it. She also uses a comb fixed into her hair arranged into a bun, kept on one side at the back of the head. Lots of hairpins of the size of scissor are used by Dongaria woman which are fixed into the hair. There is a kind of hairpin which is U-shaped and pinned in the hair locks along with the scissor-like hairpins.

ORNAMENTS

Both male and female Dongarias use different types of ornaments which consist of rings, necklaces, armlets, etc. Both men and women do tattooing on their body. A Dongaria woman with her traditional dress and ornaments is recognised easily from a crowd of women belonging to other tribal groups.

MUSICAL INSTRUMENTS

The Dongaria Kondhs use single membrane drums of different types, clapper series, cymbals and flutes. Generally men use the musical instruments and the women dance to the tune of instruments. Some musical instruments belong to the community whereas others are individually owned. For example, *dapu* is a single membrane drum which belongs to the community and is played on occasions of communal festivals like *Meria* festival. On the other hand *niseni* is also a single membrane drum. Sometimes some individuals have such drums. When the instrument is purchased a ritual is performed by the *beju* inside the house before its use. This drum is used both in communal festivals as well as in festivals performed in individual houses.

RELIGIOUS OBJECTS

The Dongaria Kondhs have shrines for different deities. *Jatra Kudi* is one such shrine located in some convenient place of the village street. The *Jatra Kudi* comprises wooden stumps arranged in position on wooden pillars, which help the deity to rest above the ground. Similarly, there is a *Kudi* which is called *Jakir Kudi*. The deity which is installed in this *Kudi* is called Father *Penu*.

Besides these shrines, the Dongarias have sacrificial posts to which the animal is tied and later sacrificed.

The Malia Kondh

Settlement Patterns and House Types

The Malia village is located in the plains close to their paddy fields. It is characterized by east-west setting of the rows of houses so that every household gets sunlight. It has a warm side in winter so that the inmates of a house sit on this side in winter and remain engaged in various occupations. Also being set on a slope, the rain water never stagnates anywhere in the street and keeps it clean. Moreover, the sunlight in other seasons keeps the street dry.

The youth dormitories are attached to the rows of houses unlike those which are built behind the rows among the Dongaria Kondhs. The dormitories which are built by the Malias are meant for the women and they have no dormitory for the boys. But the Kutia Kondhs have dormitories both for the men and for the women separately.

The cattlesheds are not built separately among the Malia Kondhs as is the practice among the Dongarias and the Kutias. The cattle are kept at night in a screened-off portion of the living room inside the house so that they get the warmth of the house and are protected against attack by the tigers.

Besides these huts there are *Meria* posts fixed into the ground in convenient places in the village street. There are three shrines located in different places in the village street. They are one for the Central *Dharani* installed at the central place of a village street, the other one for the upper *Dharani* located at the higher side at one end of the village, and the third one for the lower *Dharani* installed at the lower side and at the lower end of the village.

There are kitchen gardens behind the rows of houses all fenced properly so that the cattle and other animals do not destroy the crops. Every Malia village is generally located near a spring so that the people get water without walking long distances to fetch water. There may be a few families of Domb community in every Malia village. These houses form a separate cluster located at a little distance from the Kondh houses, but in the same site of the Malia village.

A grazing ground common to all households is located in the village boundary which is close to the scrub jungle belonging to the village. Every village has a cremation ground which is located away from the village. There are good lands used as paddy fields of different households all around the village.

There may be educational institutions such as primary schools and high schools and club houses provided by the Government. Similarly, there may be tube wells and open wells provided either by governmental agencies or privately owned. Stationery or grocery shops are present in some villages all belonging to local Oriya families.

MALIA KONDH HOUSE

A Malia Kondh house is rectangular in shape. It is a single-roomed house with inside space partitioned into separate quarters used for different purposes. The main room which occupies the central space has a space on its left side for storage of paddy bins. By its side on the same side is a place used as the middle room for various purposes. The storage shelf over the fire place and the kitchen are present on the left side separated by a partition wall from the space used for storage of paddy bins. The kitchen side partition wall has a raised platform on the ground close to the partition wall which is used for keeping water and other pots. In the space occupied by the kitchen lies the sacrificial spot. In one corner of the kitchen room lies the space where the ancestors live. A small raised platform is provided in this corner for the ancestors.

On the right side of the main room the space is used as the cattle byre. This space is set apart for the cattle to stay at night. It is separated from the remaining space of the main room by sticking wooden posts on to the ground so that no cattle can enter the sleeping quarters in the main room. Close to these posts lies the hearth on the side of the living space and the grain pounding hole is present at the centre of the main room.

The house is provided with verandahs — one in front and the other at the back. The front verandah is mud-packed and with overhanging eaves. The back verandah which is enclosed is divided into three parts — the portion on the left side is used as the pig sty and one of the remaining two portions which are on the right side is used as the women's sleeping room as and when necessary particularly during menstruation period, and the other portion which is on the extreme right is used as the fowl pen.

The house is provided with two doors, one in front opening to the front verandah and the other at the back opening to the backside of the house where the outdoor grain pounding hole is present. Except these two doors there are no windows provided in the house. The front verandah runs parallel to the front street (*raha*) of the village and beyond the back verandah lies the backyard used as the kitchen garden.

Household Objects

BADUDI (BROOM)

The Malia Kondhs like the Kutia Kondhs use twigs of a wild grass to make the brooms. This grass is available in rainy season and in winter the women collect the grass in bundles. The broom is used for sweeping the floor of the house.

KOLU (MORTAR & PESTLE)

The pestle is made of wood the forehalf of which is greater in girth and rounded in shape. The bottom half is rounded so that it can be held with a firm grip comfortably. An iron ring is fitted at the husking end.

The mortar is generally placed in the living room. The housewife while husking spreads both her legs along the side of the hole into which the mortar is fixed and releases the pressure of the pestle on the grains inside the whole using both her hands by turn.

NIJU GANA (A WOODEN OIL PRESS)

The oil press consists of two heavy planks of wood. One end of both the planks is inserted into the holes of a post. The wooden post holds the planks one above the other both horizontally placed slightly above the ground. The other ends of the planks are placed on a V-shaped pole. Both the posts (*plau*) are made of *mahua* wood. A handle (*tlau*) is fixed at the free end of the upper plank. On the side of the lower plank wood is scooped out to make a narrow channel for the oil to flow through. The press is made jointly by a group of Malias. The planks and posts are given the required shape by using axe and chisel.

The press is used for extracting oil from *mahua* seeds. The seeds are first pounded and then fried. These fried flour of the seeds are kept in small baskets which are placed in-between the planks. After that the upper plank is pressed. As a result the oil comes out of the fried flour of the seeds and flows down into the receptacle kept on the ground.

Besides these three objects there are many other important objects found in the house of a Malia Kondh. These are as follows: *tambi* (measuring bowl), *dandi* (beaker), *jumbi* (earthen pot), *laka* (gourd container), *kele* (knife), *kude* (knife), *sechu* (knife), *gasa* (ladle), *satuki* (ladle), *martadi* (hammer).

BASKETRY

The Malia Kondhs have many types of baskets which are used for storing things. They have also baskets in which they store paddy grains. They also use a kind of basket which is used as bird's cage.

Most of the baskets are made of bamboo splits which are woven using different patterns. When a bird's cage is made flexible bamboo wicks are used. These wicks criss-cross each other diagonally and leave numerous holes diagonally in-between. The bird's cage is used for keeping pet birds.

The basket which is used for keeping small fish is of check pattern and it is semi-rectangular in shape. The body is hollow and is narrowed down gradually up to the other ends. Its mouth is very small and rounded in shape. The basket is used for keeping and carrying fish home after catching from the stream and waterlogged ponds.

FOOD QUEST

The Malia Kondhs are generally agriculturists. They carry out cultivation of paddy in plain lands which are close to their villages. To carry out cultivation they use cattle drawn ploughs fitted with yokes. They also use pick and mattock to dig earth wherever necessary in the paddy fields. They use spades mainly for different earth work such as making bunds in agricultural fields, digging pits, spreading earth for levelling the ground. Earth levellers are also used to level the ground after ploughing the paddy fields before transplantation of paddy seedling takes place. The leveller also picks at weeds and wild grass, rendering the field clear of the weeds. The Malia Kondhs use sickle to harvest the crop.

HUNTING

The main hunting implements are bow and arrow, spear and axe. There is nothing special in regard to the material aspects of these implements. They are the same as those used by the other two sections of the Kondhs.

FISHING

The Malia Kondhs generally catch fish in their paddy fields and for this purpose they use traps. A fish trap has a wide open mouth narrowed down towards the closing end. Strong bamboo sticks are held vertically in a line and tied with *siali* creepers. The mouth is kept wide open by means of a strong weft wrapped round its border and tied to the sticks by a string. The narrow end is kept closed. In rainy season the trap is placed near a small stream. The mouth of the trap is directed against the flow of the stream. The women use the trap for catching fish from the agricultural fields.

BIRD CATCHING

The Malia Kondhs are in the habit of catching birds. For this purpose they use glued sticks just like those of the Kutia Kondhs. These glued sticks are set here and there in the branches of the trees during fruiting time. While the birds fly into the trees they perch on the sticks which make them unable to fly and escape. The Malia Kondhs also use various types of traps to catch birds. Loop traps of the type used by the Kutia Kondhs are very common.

The study of the material objects used by the different sections of the Kondh tribe shows that the implements used in the food quest among the Kutia Kondhs are simple. But these objects used by the Dongaria Kondhs and Malia Kondhs are found to be much more elaborate and numerous. But certain devices which are used for catching birds and animals are very common among the three sections of the tribe.

Personal Care, Dress and Adornments

DRESS

The dress of both men and women among the Malia Kondhs is just like that of neighbouring Hindus. The men wear *dhoti* and shirt and the women wear *sari* and blouse. Red and blue coloured sarees are their favourite costumes. The women arrange their hair into a bun, kept in position at the back of the head by means of hairpins.

The Malia women are fond of wearing various types of ornaments which include earrings, hairpins, silver bangles, anklets, neck bands, etc.

Tattooing is most common among the Malia Kondh women. They get their face, hands and legs tattooed with dots and lines.

RELIGIOUS OBJECTS

Jakiri is their village deity consisting of a wooden post. It is made by communal effort by all the villagers of a Malia village. Men, not women, shape the wood to make a *Jakiri* post. *Jakiri* is worshipped by the village priest and buffalo is sacrificed as a part of worship.

The Malia Kondhs have also sacrificial posts called *koru koba*. A post is carved out towards its upper half into three sections. It is posted before the village deity and used at the time of communal offering of buffalo and other animals to the deity.

MUSICAL INSTRUMENTS

The Malia Kondhs use single membrane drum called *dala*. The drum is very heavy and therefore it is hung by means of a piece of rope from a wood carried by two men on their shoulders while the man at the back beats the drum by two drum sticks. They also use membrane phone which is a circular shaped hollow piece of wood. While playing it the user holds it by the left hand and beats the right palm on the membrane. The sound emitted along with the rattling of the rings varies in pitch in accordance with the degree of tension the membrane gets.

Glossary

Kutia Kondhs

Akagiri Deba	:	Back door
Ali Tangi	:	Axe
Ambu	:	Arrow
Asang Gurudu	:	Duck pen
Attu	:	Ceiling
Baber	:	A kind of grass (*Eulalipsis binata*)
Bahar Tati	:	Shutter made of bamboo splits
Basi	:	Flute
Becha	:	Bow string
Behari Deba	:	Double-panelled wooden door
Burla	:	Small grain bin
Chatu	:	Ladle (Mara set)
Chhatia	:	Messenger-cum-cattle herder
Dadam	:	Single membrane drum
Damani	:	A kind of wood (*Grewia liciacfolia*)
Dapa	:	Elevated platforms of a house
Darubali	:	The stone which is laid down half buried in the ground
Daska Kudi	:	Spinsters' dormitory
Dehu Penu	:	Deity guarding the village
Deri Kare	:	Knife
Dharani Penu	:	Earth Goddess
Dharani Vali	:	Mother Goddess

Dua Duna	:	Tobacco Container
Duabali	:	Stone on which tobacco leaves are powdered
Eja	:	Living room
Guani	:	Fish trap
Gunjer Bali	:	Quern
Jaka	:	Back verandah
Janging	:	Clapper
Jani	:	The magico-religious head of the village
Jaruki	:	A type of wood (*Grewia tiliaefolia*)
Jhatra	:	Broom
Juali	:	Yoke
Kabda Lauri	:	Dried fruit with seeds inside making sonorous or rattle sound
Kabda	:	One type of local plant
Kacha	:	Basket used for carrying paddy
Kadeli	:	String cot
Kadi Gutra	:	A wooden device to which bullocks are trained in ploughing
Kagda	:	Neck ornaments
Kaju Sipa Dituri	:	Birds cage
Kaju, Ada Ilu	:	Goat and poultry pen
Kajukuting	:	Snare for catching wild fowl
Kallu	:	Pestle
Kalu	:	Finger ring
Kama	:	Aeolian flute
Kapa Sikiding	:	Hairpin
Kasada Mada	:	Hairpin
Kataku	:	The diviner for conducting a special kind of ritual
Kepa Basuli	:	Adze
Khapars	:	Clay tiles

Kin Kichadi	:	Earring
Koding Sala	:	Cow shed
Korumunda	:	Sacrificial post/*Meria* pole
Kreti	:	Silver ladle
Kudi	:	Shaft
Kudu	:	Small handle of Terka Danga
Kulinga Gadi	:	Large grain bin
Kuradi	:	Axe
Kurli Pade	:	Leveller
Kuti	:	Small wooden peg
Lahabali	:	Upper surface of the grinding stone
Langel	:	Plough
Madang Dana	:	Leaf cup
Mahuli	:	A kind of liquor
Majhi	:	Village headman
Mani Duna	:	Bamboo container
Maning bei	:	Fence made of thick bamboo splits
Maso Parang Titudi	:	Gourd container
Meria	:	One kind of important festival
Mini	:	Bamboo reed
Minu Kare	:	Knife
Muang Lauri	:	A musical instrument of pellet-bells or hollow rattle type
Mutha Majhi	:	In charge of collecting revenue from the people
Muti	:	Bottom haft
Nakudi Danga	:	Wooden trough in which dogs eat
Nanka Begi	:	Pellet bag
Pabaveru/Jagdi	:	Field huts
Padar Puja	:	One kind of festival

Paik	:	A caste
Pajing Danga	:	Wooden trough from which pigs eat
Pajing Soleng	:	Pig sty
Palka Gatra	:	Sickle
Papi	:	Loft
Pareni	:	Iron ring
Phade	:	Stool
Pijurudangar	:	Kutia God
Pikasi	:	Pick and mattock
Punikalu	:	One kind of festival
Rasa Padangi	:	Bangles
Sadani Tinei	:	Sago palm container
Sargi	:	*Sal* wood
Satrangi	:	One type of plant which is used for broom making
Sela	:	Mat
Serbebali/ Merabali	:	Curry-stone
Siali Creeper	:	*Bauhinia vahlii*
Sika Ditory	:	Bag used for keeping small objects like coins and ornaments
Simba Dapra	:	Ladle for serving gruel
Sindul Duna	:	Gum sticks
Sindul	:	One type of gum
Siperi	:	The broom made out of a plant called *satrangi* (grass)
Takna	:	Flat basket used for drying *ragi*, millets and seeds
Taku Puja	:	One kind of festival
Tangi	:	Axe
Tati	:	Shutters
Tatkad	:	Cow bell

Terka Danga	:	A wooden device for pounding bamboo shoots
Timba Dedi	:	Wooden deity
Toderi	:	Waist belt
Vitrieja	:	Kitchen
Wilu	:	Bow

Dongaria Kondhs

Ada	:	Measuring bowl
Ada Hada	:	Goat pen
Adisbeta	:	Spinsters' dormitory
Ambu	:	Arrow
Badti	:	Lamp stand used in the shrine at home
Banjeli	:	Basket for hanging it from the loft
Barik	:	Who calls people to attend the village meeting
Bejuni	:	Black art/magician of the village
Ber Penu	:	Inside view of the shrine
Bismajhi	:	Assistant to *Jani*
Damani	:	One type of wood
Dapa	:	Back verandah
Dappu	:	Single membrane drum made from goat's skin
Daura	:	Talisman
Dehuri	:	Medicine man
Dipi	:	Hanging lamp stand
Dumuni	:	Serving ladle
Eja	:	Living room
Father Penu Jakir kudi	:	Wall paintings inside the shrine
Gajjeri	:	Spear
Ghata Penu Kudi	:	The view of the shrine
Gininga	:	Cymbals

Gorada : Shrine

Gouda : Gouda takes the cattle to graze and brings back

Gunch : Pellet bow

Guruti : Bird's cage

Hanguni : Basket used for keeping vegetables

Hatudi : Bamboo leaf hat

Hikeri : One type of wood

Hitki : Basket used for covering meat or fish while drying them in the sun

Holu : Oven

Ichun Kdali : Small axe

Jani : Village priest

Janjinga : Clapper series

Jata Bali : Grinding stone

Jatra Kudi : Shrine of the goddess located at the entrance to the village

Jatrakudi Penu : This god installed in a hut at the outskirts of the village

Jhatuni : *Jhatuni* sweeps the village street and keeps it clean and serve as mediators in business transactions.

Kading Hada : Cowshed

Kagudi : Necklace

Kaja Kdali : Adze

Kakawa : Comb made of buffalo horn

Kakawa Badga : The wooden stamp which is required for *Kakawa*

Kakuya : Wooden comb

Kalu : Pestle

Kapda ganda : Dongaria women's clothes

Kaska Kuda : Poultry pen

Katei Bali : Sacrificial post

Kedu	:	A festival in which buffalo is sacrificed
Khanda	:	Sword
Kilamodi	:	Hairpin
Kodi	:	Dongaria male's clothes
Kolu Munda	:	Wooden club; Ceremonial club
Kotebali Penu	:	Dongaria God installed by the side of *Dharani Penu*
Kudi	:	Hut of the Earth Goddess; Shrine
Kudilinga	:	Tattooing
Kuta	:	Axe
Kutikera	:	Bamboo stick
Kwte	:	Earpin
Ladi Guda	:	Field hut
Mada Kalu	:	Beaker
Madi Duna	:	Bamboo container
Mana	:	Measuring wooden bowl
Mandal	:	Headman of the *Mutha*
Matra	:	Containing grains
Mila Kdali	:	Small axe
Mlallu Duka	:	Rabbit's Trap
Mudla	:	A wooden hammer
Muli	:	Blacksmith
Munda	:	A wooden stump which is used for locking the door.
Mutha	:	A socio-political organization
Niseni	:	Single membrane drum made from cow's hide.
Pajing Kuda	:	Pig sty
Palka	:	Teeth of the comb which is made from buffalo horn
Pipel Katri	:	Small knife

Pipli : Tiny knife
Pitda Dipi : Lamp used in the living room
Pujari : One of the functionaries whose axe falls first on the *meria* animal during *meria* sacrifice.
Simini : Hatchet
Simne : A typical axe
Sipna : Hairpin
Sunga : Tobacco pipe for men
Sungha : Tobacco pipe for women
Suri : Knife
Surudi : Flute
Tadwa : Armlet
Tahapa : Hoe
Takurani : Lamp post
Tatkadi : Cowbell
Thakurani : Goddesses
Unga Katra : Basket used for collecting minor forest produce
Watimuna : Pellet bag
Weg : Sickle
Welu : Bow

Malia Kondhs

Ambu : Arrow
Arki : One type of liquor
Badudi : A type of wild grass with which brooms are made
Bala : Silver Bangles
Binjuri : Basket for keeping things
Birigagali : Anklet
Buda Deba : Large grain bin
Burki : *Siali* strings

Daadi	:	Loft
Dagari	:	U-shaped iron hook used in yoke
Dala Kila	:	Two drum sticks used for beating the drum
Dala	:	Single membrane drum
Dandi	:	Beaker
Dangeli	:	Basket for keeping things
Dharani	:	Worship of *Dharani Penu*
Depang Pati	:	Bars of the house
Diudi	:	Small basket for keeping tiny fish
Dula	:	Bars
Gaheli	:	Cowshed
Garka	:	Spear
Gasa	:	Ladle
Gazurka	:	A type of wild bush used for thatching the roof
Giredi	:	Fish trap
Gogla	:	Neck band
Guda	:	Bird's cage
Ija	:	Living room
Irpi Besku	:	A type of wood called *Mahua*
Jakiri	:	Village deity
Jani	:	Ritual head of the village
Jueli	:	Yoke
Jumbi	:	Earthen pot
Kaati	:	Tile frame
Kada	:	The beam of the earth leveller
Kada	:	The beam of the plough
Kadangija	:	Kitchen
Kadangkudi	:	Room divider (partition)
Kanda	:	Small wooden bars used for the roof
Kanjari	:	Membrane phone

Kedu Parba	:	A kind of festival
Kehele	:	Sickle
Kele	:	Knife for cutting branches of trees and for fencing
Khapars	:	Fired clay tiles used for the roof
Kichedka	:	Earring
Kilanga	:	Wooden pegs of the yoke
Kloju	:	Wooden handle of axe
Kolu	:	Pestle
Koru Koba	:	The sacrificial wooden post
Kotebali	:	A male deity Dharani Penu's husband
Korvbanga	:	Door frames
Kude	:	Knife for cutting things
Kudu	:	The walls of all the four sides of a house
Kujanga	:	Bird's trap
Kumbhar	:	Potter
Kurli	:	Earth leveller
Kuti	:	Peg holding a beam
Laka	:	Gourd container
Lauska	:	Spinster's dormitory
Likudi	:	Chisel
Madipati	:	Bamboo splints
Makidinga	:	Smaller wooden posts which are used for safety of the roof
Martadi	:	Hammer
Mutha	:	The largest territorial unit of Malia Kondh
Mutti	:	The grip of the broom
Nachakoba	:	Corner pillars of the door
Nangeli Laha	:	The pointed iron share of the *Nangeli* plough
Nangeli	:	Plough

Niju Gana	:	A wooden oil press
Paerdorr	:	Strings of *siali* creeper
Pangedka	:	Wooden planks
Paredi	:	Iron ring used for the grip
Pata	:	Doors
Patasingh	:	Earth leveller
Pikasi	:	Pick and mattock
Plau	:	Posts of the oil press
Pujari	:	Village priest who also presides over the *Meria* festival
Pujupaka	:	Hairpin
Rapa	:	Spade
Sanga	:	Single membrane drum
Sardar	:	Headman of Mutha
Satuki	:	Ladle
Sechu Knife	:	Knife used for cutting things
Sedi Kamanga	:	Horns made of brass
Sindhi Malu	:	Date palm tree
Sindu Kdalu	:	Glued sticks for catching birds
Solu	:	Hearth
Tabedi	:	Wooden beams
Tabedra	:	Side walls are called *Tabedra*
Talikudu	:	Side walls
Tambi	:	Measuring bowl
Tangari	:	Axe
Tlau	:	A handle which is fixed at the free end of the upper plank
Tulipati	:	Supporting ridge pole
Wilu	:	Bow

Reference Literature

Anonymous, *The Kondhs of Hill Tribes*, Calcutta, vol. V (1846), pp. 22-85.

Ali, Almas, "Health and Genetic Problems of Kutia Khonds of Barlubara Village," *Adibasi*, vol. XVIII, nos. 1-4, (1978-79), pp. 56-62.

Bailey, F.G., *Caste and Economic Frontier*, London: Oxford University Press, 1985.

———, *Tribe, Caste and Nation,* London: Oxford University Press, 1960.

———, "Political Charge in Kondhmals," *Eastern Anthropologist*, vol. 11, no. 2 (1958), pp. 58-106.

Banerjee, Sukumar, *Ethnographic Study of the Kui-Kondh*, Calcutta: Anthropological Survey of India, 1969.

Behura, N.K., "Transformation of Human Sacrifice Among the Khonds of Orissa," *Vanyajati*, vol. X (1962), pp. 93-99.

———, "Oaths, Ordeals and Divination Among the Desia Kondhs of Orissa," *Vanyajati*, vol. XVII, no. 2 (1969).

———, *Life and Development of the Dongaria Kondhs in Niyamgiri Hills*, Souvenir Adibasi Exhibition, Bhubaneswar, 1985, pp. 34-38.

Boal, Barbara M., *The Konds, Human* Sacrifice *and Religious Change*, Bhubaneswar: Modern Book Depot, 1984.

Das Patnaik, P.S. & Sarat Das, "A Comparative Analysis of the Cognitive Abilites of Unschooled Children of Bonda and Dongaria Kondh of Koraput District," *Adibasi,* vol. XVII, no. 1-4 (1977-78), pp. 31-42.

Devi, Kiranbala, "Kondh," *Adibasi*, vol. V, no. 3, pp. 63-64.

Devi, Bharati, "How and What the Kuvi Kondhs Adorn," *Adibasi*, vol. XVI, no. 1, (1972-73), pp. 21-26.

Elwin, Verrier, "Notes on a Kondh Town," *Man in India*, vol. XXIV, no. 1, (1944), pp. 40-50.

———, *Tribe Myths of Orissa*, Oxford University Press, 1957.

Friend-Perira, J.A., "Customs of Kondhs," *Journal of the Asiatic Society of Bengal*, vol. 71, 1902, pp. 18-28.

———, "Totemism Among the Khonds," *Journal of the Asiatic Society of Bengal*, LXXIII, 3 (1904), pp. 39-56.

———, "Some Khond Songs," *Journal of the Asiatic Society of Bengal*, LXVIII (1899), pp. 1-13.

Frye, J.P., "On the Uriya and Kondh Population of Orissa," *Journal of the Royal Asiatic Society*, XVII, (1860), pp. 1-38.

Frowde, H., Kondh the Imperial Gazetteer of India, Oxford, vol. XVI, (1908), pp. 280-88.

Hota, N.R., "Human Sacrifice Among the Khonds of Orissa," *Orissa Historical Research Journal,* vol. VIII, no. 3-4 (1959-60), pp. 158-63.

Jena, Krishnachandra, "The Kondhs of Koraput," *Indian Journal of Social Work*, XXIII, (1962-63), pp. 57-61.

Mazumdar, B.C., "The Kui or the Kondh People," *Man in India*, vol. XII, (1932) pp. 245-52.

Mishra, Baladev, "The Agricultural System, Diet and Dietary Habits of the Kondhs and Tribe of Orissa," *Vanyajati*, vol. XI (1963) pp. 135-42.

Mohanty Gopinath, "Cultural Change Among the Kuvi Kondhs," *Adibasi*, vol. II, no. 1, (1957-58), pp. 9-20.

Mukherjee, Probhat, "Human Sacrifice Among the Khonds of Orissa, A Note" *Orissa Historical Research Journal,* vol. VIII, 3-4 (1959-60), pp. 164-67.

Nandi, Santibhusan, "A Kondh Resettlement Colony, Some Aspects of its Impact on the Settlers," *Vanyajati*, vol. X, (1962) pp. 161-67.

Niggemeyer, Hermann, "Kutia Kondha Pilara Ekoisia," (Oriya), *Adibasi*, vol. 1, No. 2 & 3 (1957) pp. 5-7.

———, "The Name Giving Ceremony of the Kutia Kondh," *Adibasi*, vol. 11, no. 1 (1957-58), pp. 3-6.

Nayak, Gitanjali, "A Study of Kutia Kondhs Food," *Adibasi*, vol. XVI, no. 1 (1976) p. 16.

Panda, S., "Demography of a Kondh Village," *Adibasi*, vol. XI, no. 3 (1969-70), pp. 27-35.

Patnaik, N. & P.S. Daspatnaik, *The Kondh of Orissa*, THRTI, Bhubaneswar 1982.

Patnaik, Uma Charan, "The Kondhs of the Hills," One Century of British Rule (1836 to 1936), *Modern Review*, vol. LXXVIII (1945), pp. 214-18.

Pattanaik, Prananatha, "Phulabani Jilara Kondha Adibasi," (Oriya), *Navajivana*, vol., VII, no. 1 (1962) pp. 25-32.

Pattanaik, U.K., "Reminiscences of an Administrative Officer in the Kondha Hills," *Adibasi*, (1964-65) no. 2, pp. 29-37.

———, "Religious Ceremonies, Ordeals and a Legend About Oriya Infiltration" *Adibasi* (1969-70), no. 4, pp. 76-84.

Patel, Srisha, "ABO Blood Groups Among the Kondhs in Daringbadi (Phulbani dist)," (1972-73), pp. 64-66.

Pathey, Jagannath, "Political Economy of Kandhland," *Man in India*, vol. 56, no. 1, (1976) pp. 1-36.

Raman, Leela V., "The Kondh of Phulbani," *Adibasi*, vol. 11, no. 1 (1957-58), pp. 35-40).

Rao, L.N., "The Khonds, Tribal People of South Orissa," *Modern Review*, vol. LXVII (1940) pp. 199-200.

Ray, G.S., "A Study of the Physical Character of the Kondh," *Eastern Anthropologist*, vol. 11 (1949) pp. 130-44.

———, "Characteristic Features of Kondh Kinship Terminology," *Eastern Anthropologist*, vol. 11, (1949-50), pp. 151-57.

Ray, S.C., "Ethnography in Old Official Recorder (Kondh Human Sacrifice)" *Man in India*, vol. 11 (1922), pp. 67-81.

Rout, Siba Prasad, "Dom Exploitation in the Khond Villages of Koraput District," *Adibasi*, (1964-65) no. 1, pp. 21-28.

Russel, R.V., "Tribes Castes of Central Provinces of India," vol. 111, Part III, (1975), pp. 416-481.

Samantaray, D.K., "The Kondh of Nayagarh," *Adibasi*, vol. XII, nos. 1-4, (1970-71), pp. 22-26.

Schulze, F.V.P., *The Religion of the Kuvi Kondhs, Their Customs and Folklore*, Madras Graves Cookson and Co. (1912), p. 100.

Sharma, Krishna, *The Kondhs of Orissa*, Delhi: Concept Publishing Co., 1981.

Swain, J., "The Kondh Pantheon and their Social Significance," *Adibasi*, vol. X, no. 3 & 4 (1968-69), pp. 33-39.

Tripathy, K.C., "Taste, Mid-digital Hair and Occipital Hair-whorls of Kondhs," *Adibasi*, vol. VIII, no. 1, (1966-67) pp. 29-36.